Points.

1. AP's classical sources.

2. Problem with approach:

   AP is often at his best
   when transcending / &
   departing from the source,
   as in RL: The Care of
   Spleen & Clarissa's
   (p. 28)   M.

                              Creech's
              transl. of Manilius

3. Sources are not first Ovid's
   the usual ones but
   Manilius, Astronomica.

4. p. 31 procedure —

5. Manilius using argument
   from design to attack
   Manilius.

6. Detecting echoes of
   Ovid here, Horace
   there.

7. pp 77. Sporus — awful!
   This is what it produces.
   Example. Good
   analytic.

8. Kind of Brower redone
   30 yrs. later.

9. No Eloisa to Abelard.

"the providence of wit"
   Dryden, Epistle to Robert Howard

10. p. 103 Q. savage. Silly —
    makes no sense.

11. A quest for familiarity with
    AP's sources," p. 104.

12. 105 — AP, Ethics, Manilius, Stoicism

13. Bibliog. Brower 1969. Proof!

14. 137 — Manilean infl. again

p. 13 start.

No Weinbrot! But 1977
   secondary works.
Pope & Newton — 113

POPE ON CLASSIC GROUND

POPE ON CLASSIC GROUND

G. F. C. Plowden

"And still I seem to tread on classic ground."

Ohio University Press

Athens, Ohio

Library of Congress Cataloging in Publication Data

Plowden, G. F. C., 1929-
  Pope on classic ground.

  Bibliography: p.
  Includes index.
  1. Pope, Alexander, 1688-1744—Sources.
2. Classical literature—History and criticism.
I. Title.
PR3636.P58   1983   821'.5   82-14413
ISBN 0-8214-0664-7

Vatis Alexandri meditaris carmina parvi
  (ingenio pollens, corpore parvus erat)
et quantum valeant humanam tangere mentem,
  quantum hominum mores excoluisse, doces;
hic tibi primus amor, Musas qui diligis omnes,
  "hoc sit opus" dixit Cynthius ipse "tuum."
quare hunc accipias oro, venerande, libellum;
  te leve discipulus munus habere cupit.
nam sine te, fateor, scripta inrita nostra fuissent,
  cuncta forent sine te caeca, nec apta legi.
sic si collectas iunxisses, Daedale, pennas
  Cnosia te tegeret terra, tuumque genus,
sic vel si Paphius molem sculpsisset eburnam
  cum Paphio numquam concubuisset ebur.
non ferre hanc poteras poenam, vanosque labores
  iussisti fessa me reparare manu.
et dolui et feci. quanto sudore reportat
  adque pedes pandus ponit asellus onus!
nunc etiam remanent mendae, peioraque mendis,
  et desiderium nunc quoque fallit opus,
sed vitiis parces: nam cui lyra blanda Camenae
  cara est, et geminum quae lavat unda iugum,
huic ubi mens dubitat, falsisque ambagibus errat,
  docte vir, huic semper mitis amicus eris.

Contents

Acknowledgments

Like other students of Pope, I have been greatly helped by the labors of the Twickenham editors, and of Professor George Sherburn on Pope's correspondence. The other writers on Pope who have given me pleasure and profit are many, but I would especially mention Reuben Brower and Earl Wasserman, who have been so particularly concerned with the interpretation of Pope through his allusions.

My most important theme, which is Pope's view of the Creation, has also been treated by Professor Martin C. Battestin in *The Providence of Wit*, which I did not read until my own work in this direction was largely finished. I had already dealt in earlier drafts with all the passages that Professor Battestin and I both discuss. In fact, because of the difference in approach, I believe that the two studies duplicate each other only a little.

My thanks to Professor Maynard Mack have already been expressed. I must also thank other friends who have read and commented on my manuscripts, including especially Professor R. G. M. Nisbet, who, generous as ever with his time and learning, has given me encouragement and reassurance in my dealings with classical matters.

Texts and References

For Pope I have used the Twickenham edition, which is the only modern edition to print the *Epistle to Cobham* without the changes that Warburton persuaded Pope to adopt. For Sandys's Ovid I have used the fourth edition, of 1632. For Creech's Manilius I have used the first edition, of 1697; but all the editions seem to be identical. For classical works I have used the volumes in the Loeb library, which will probably be the most convenient for readers. For other works, I have used convenient good editions. Details of the works cited are given in the bibliographical list.

The spelling has been slightly modernized by the adoption of the present-day usage for the letters "j" and "v."

In references to classical works when large Roman numerals are used for the book number then the line numbers given refer to the Greek or Latin original. When small Roman numerals are used the line numbers refer to the translation.

There is some difficulty in giving references to Sandys's Ovid because of the lack of line numbers and because of variations in page numbers between editions. I have given the page numbers of the fourth edition. Readers will probably be able to find the place in other editions without too much difficulty. In references to Creech's Manilius I have given the page numbers, which are the same in all editions. Creech has three series of page numbers, one for the preface, one for the first three books, and one for the last two.

All the quotations from Manilius are from Creech's translation, except for one or two that I specify as being by Sherburne. Any unattributed prose translations of Greek or Latin extracts are my own.

CHAPTER 1

Introduction

One of the great difficulties and also pleasures of reading Pope is that he conveys so much through allusion and imitation. The difficulty may arise from the subtlety of his means, demanding from us the same minute attention by which, Johnson tells us, he formed his notions; we may fail for years to notice in familiar lines echoes of familiar texts. Then again, he often alludes to works that are now forgotten and perhaps were never very well known even to his contemporaries. The purpose of this book is to increase our understanding of his poetry by examining certain connected groups of his borrowings, from a comparatively small number of sources, which have hitherto remained almost unnoticed. At the beginning, some space has also been given to an elaborate borrowing in the *Rape of the Lock*. Although this borrowing contributes little or nothing to the interpretation of the poem, it may be of interest for what it reveals both about Pope's methods and about the way a great artist can strike from chance, using the materials that fall to his hand.

A few books that will be referred to here may require some brief introduction. The first is George Sandys's *Ovid's Metamorphosis*, which first appeared in 1626. The translation itself is, of course, fairly well known and has often been discussed in connection with Pope, especially in Volume I of the Twickenham edition. Pope scholars have paid much less attention to the notes, roughly equal to the text in length, which first came out in the

1

fourth edition of 1632 and were reprinted in 1640. They interpret Ovid in the light of contemporary thought and scholarship and contain a good deal of Sandys's own varied knowledge of the world. On the whole Sandys's notes are lively and interesting in spite of their moralizing and allegorizing, which in those days could not be dispensed with, it seems, however remote from the poet's purpose the interpretation may have been. Pope, who praised Sandys's learning as well as his skill as a translator, knew the work well, as his writings show. For example, one of the things he seems to have had in mind when he wrote his lines on the development of society in *Essay on Man*, Epistle III, lines 241 ff., was Sandys's allegorization of Phaethon as the type of the rash prince; and, as often, there is a verbal clue in the resemblance of line 290, "Taught not to slack, nor strain its tender strings," to Sandys's words "as *Apollonius* answered *Adrian*, that *Nero* lost his empire by the sometimes overstraining, and sometimes too much slacking the strings of his instrument" (p. 67).

Sandys's notes contain, rendered into different meters, many illustrative extracts from the poets, and several of them seem to have caught Pope's eye. One even has its own modest place in literary history, for it is apparently the first translation in heroic couplets of Sarpedon's speech to Glaucus in Book XII of the Iliad and it influenced Denham's translation, which Pope admired.

A less-known work, but one very interesting for Pope scholars, is Manilius's *Astronomica*, a poem of the late Augustan period, of which over four thousand lines, in five books, survive. Book I is mainly astronomical description, Books II and III and part of Book IV concern themselves with fairly technical astrology, and part of Book IV and all of Book V are given up to character sketches of the various signs of the zodiac and other constellations. Manilius was a Stoic, and there are philosophical passages in the first four books, especially at the beginning of Book I and at the end of Book IV. There are also some embellishments, notably a would-be Ovidian narrative in Book V, which we shall shortly meet. The poem is highly derivative, badly constructed, and even to a layman's eye scientifically inaccurate and incomplete; how-

ever, the versification and style are not contemptible, even if the wit is a trifle mechanical. One might trace a Manilian influence on Pope's style in phrases like "truth itself's a lie," which employ extreme yet not startling paradoxes. As an opponent, however poetically unequal, of Lucretius's atheism, Manilius seems to have offered some attractions for the seventeenth and early eighteenth centuries, and some passages, especially in Book I, were apparently quite well known. Many modern readers would enjoy the characters, which give a picture of Roman life not quite like anything to be found elsewhere and would probably be well known if the rest of the poem had not survived to deter readers.

The first important work on Manilius in England was Sir Edward Sherburne's volume *The Sphere of Marcus Manilius*, a magnificent folio of 1675, which contains a dignified translation of Book I and copious notes and appendices. Sherburne shows an impressive knowledge of literature, philosophy, and science, and some acquaintance with six or seven Oriental languages. It seems safe to assume that Pope would have known this book (the Harleian had a copy) but I have not found positive evidence that he did.

Thomas Creech, whose earlier translation of Lucretius had been successful with the public, brought out a complete translation, accompanied by a preface and notes, in 1697. It must have had some success, for it was reprinted in 1700, 1714, and 1722, apparently usually in one volume with his Lucretius. It is not consistently close to the Latin, and it is full of supplementary material from related passages of the classics and sometimes apparently from Creech's own head, especially when, as often, the text was corrupt. Creech quite often imitates Dryden, as when he ends his translation of a short passage about the Odyssey from Book II with "And willing Nations knew their Native Lord." This is almost the same as the line from *Absalom and Achitophel* that Pope used unchanged to conclude his Homer: "And willing Nations knew their Lawful Lord." Thus while Pope's borrowing was from Dryden, Creech seems to have prompted it. It is worth reproducing Spence's anecdote of 1736 showing Pope's opinion about Creech and Manilius:

> Creech hurt his translation of Lucretius very much by imitat-
> ing Cowley, and bringing in turns even into some of the most
> grand parts. He has done more justice to Manilius than he has to
> Lucretius.
>
> "That was much easier to do?" [asked Spence]. That's true. —
> No, he could never be of the high age (speaking of Manilius).

Pope, who owned a copy, took a good deal from Creech, always, of
course, improving it vastly. An example may be given of a Manilian phrase turned into a good line by Creech and into a very good
one by Pope. Manilius has "dum quaerimus aevum perdimus"
(IV, 3-4), which Creech translates, "And seeking how to Live, con-
sume a Life." In Pope's hands this becomes, "And die of nothing
but a Rage to live" (*Epistle to a Lady*, 100).

No doubt because Pope used his borrowings to illustrate typical ideas rather than quote particular authors, he was not concerned with the unfaithfulnesses of the translators, and there is no
great need for us to be. Hence, when I attribute something to, say,
the *Metamorphoses* or the *Astronomica*, or perhaps even to Ovid
or Manilius by name, it may only mean that it is to be found in the
translation, not in the Latin.

Pope also owned a copy of the third edition, published in
1701, of the poet Thomas Stanley's *The History of Philosophy*, an
encyclopedic work that had originally appeared in the middle of
the seventeenth century. The work is on a vast scale, as may be
judged from the fact that the chapter on Socrates contains a verse
translation of Aristophanes's *Clouds*. Stanley recounts a good
deal of legend, but he is not wholly uncritical, and he even pro-
poses a number of emendations of his sources. It seems clear that
Pope knew parts, at least, of this book quite well. He had also read
Stanley's *History of the Chaldaick Philosophy*, which was often
bound in the same volume, and which contains an account of
"dæmons," some, but not all, of whose nocturnal activities were
transferred to the sylphs in the *Rape of the Lock*.

The last of these books is the *Thesaurus Graecae Linguae*

published by Henri Estienne "le Grand," or Stephanus, in 1572. A monument of humanist learning, it remained the standard lexicon for centuries. All well-furnished libraries would have had it, and Pope, or anybody else with a lasting interest in Greek, would have used it. The 1572 edition is not arranged in strict alphabetical order, but in etymological groupings. One head word is chosen for each root, and all other words derived from the same root follow. The longer articles therefore become almost like essays in Greek thought. One can trace the influence of certain articles of the *Thesaurus* on Pope, and there is at least one important concept that he seems to have obtained from it, as I shall try to show.

CHAPTER 2

The Rape of a Myth

Literature can surely show no finer example of an opportunity seized than the *Rape of the Lock*. Pope, by his own account to Spence, had been asked by his friend John Caryll for a poem to "laugh together again" the Fermors and the Petres, who were estranged because Lord Petre had removed a lock of Miss Arabella Fermor's hair, and he produced the first draft in 1711 in less than a fortnight. This was the genesis of the work that soon won the admiration of the public and has always kept it, even when Pope's reputation was at its lowest ebb. Caryll, who had probably expected little more than an epigram or some other well-turned trifle, should have been well satisfied with the literary result of his request, even if it did not achieve its practical aim.

We cannot, of course, know exactly how Pope approached his task during that well-spent fortnight, but we may be certain of at least one thing, he would have looked for classical parallels to the incident he was celebrating, hoping that they would yield some amusing comparison or contrast. We find allusions to Catullus's poem on Berenice's lock, and to Scylla and Nisus in the *Metamorphoses*, and epigraphs on cut hair from Ovid and Martial. But there is one episode from the *Metamorphoses* which we should expect to see reflected, since it is almost a *locus classicus* for hair: the story of the Gorgon Medusa, who was punished for profaning the temple of Minerva by having her beautiful tresses turned to snakes. Since she later lost them all, head and all, to a

7

hero, the story may have seemed to offer scope for Pope's wit.
These lines of Sandys's from near the end of Book IV, spoken by
Perseus at the banquet for his rescue of Andromeda, might almost
have been written about Belinda herself:

> Her passing beauty was the onely scope
> Of mens affections, and their envied hope:
> Yet was not any part of her more rare
> (So say they who have seene her) then her haire.
>
>   [IV, 794-797; p. 151]

We seem to hear a distant echo of them in the *Rape of the Lock*:

> This Nymph, to the Destruction of Mankind,
> Nourish'd two Locks, which graceful hung behind
> . . . .
> Love in these Labyrinths his Slaves detains.
>
>   [II, 19-20, 23]

The story of Medusa in Ovid is embedded in the story of Perseus and Andromeda and would have led Pope to it. This chapter
will attempt to show that the narrative of the *Rape of the Lock* is
modeled on that of the slaying of the monster by Perseus, of the
victory banquet that followed, and of the fight that interrupted
the banquet. The matter is complicated by the fact that for the
earlier parts of the poem Pope relied mainly on Book V of
Creech's Manilius, where the story of Andromeda is also told,
rather than on Ovid. Of course, Pope had to metamorphose all
this alien material most thoroughly, but enough evidence remains to prove the case.

The *Rape of the Lock* as it appeared in the first edition in
1712 was, of course, very different from the poem we read today. It
was less than half the length and lacked the sylphs, the game of
ombre, and the visit to the Cave of Spleen. The story line is
simpler and corresponds more directly to that of the myth, as
readers who so wish will be able to see from the material that will
be provided. Some of the later additions were drawn from the
myth, but not all; and the sylphs in particular seem to owe little or

nothing to it. Thus, since Canto I is largely devoted to the sylphs, the main Andromeda borrowing, which in 1712 began after about the first twenty lines of the poem, does not now begin until Canto II. However, the toilet scene at the end of Canto I appears to have been suggested partly by a passage from Manilius's account of Cassiopeia, the constellation that immediately precedes Andromeda. It is convenient to examine this subsidiary borrowing first.

> When mourning *Cassiopeia*, grac'd with Stars,
> Upon the left hand of the *Youth* appears,
> And joins twice ten Degrees, her Beams impart
> In Metals skill, and fill the Births with Art:
> The precious Matter they shall nobly mold,
> And raise the native value of the Gold;
> Hence shine our Temples, and our Roman *Jove*
> Fills here a Heaven as bright as that above;
> Happy this Art employ'd on things Divine,
> To frame a Statue, or adorn a Shrine;
> But now how low her Head she strives to hide,
> Whilst chain'd to Luxury, and a Slave to pride!
> Now precious Metals common Roofs enfold,
> Rival the Temples, and we feast in Gold.
> But great *Augustus* doth its state maintain,
> Shews its old worth, and makes it rise again;
> His Temples shine, and now such Works are wrought
> As *Mithridates* lost when *Sylla* fought;
> The Sun's outshone, and *Caesar*'s glorious Gems
> Excel the native lustre of his Beams:
> And hence with joy we view that wondrous Prize,
> The Monuments of *Pompey*'s Victories;
> Though those did first a Lust for Gems inspire,
> Which still burns new, and spreads a growing fire;
> The Ornaments of Kings now serve to grace
> A shape, and raise the value of a Face;
> Now Neck, Feet, Hands are deckt, and every Dress
> Shines with the Spoils of groaning Provinces;
> Yet 'tis the *Ladies* Sign, their wants supply'd
> Advance its worth, they love what decks their Pride:
> Lest want of Matter should the Work restrain,

The Art grow idle, and the *Sign* be vain,
By the same Powers are wretched Men decoy'd
To dig for Oar, and work to be employ'd;
To turn the Globe to search where Metals breed,
And see young *Gold* first blushing in its Seed;
Harmless it lies, 'till the mistaken worth
Deludes poor Man, and brings the Monster forth.
And lest Temptations too obscure should lye,
To far remov'd from every common Eye,
Mixt with the Sands they shine on every Shore,
These he shall gather, and extract the Oar,
Or dive for Jewels, and, intent on Gain,
Pierce thro the Floods, and search the deepest Main;
Draw Gold and Silver from the Waves embrace,
And work them singly, and adorn the Mass;
Or in *Electrum* both ignobly join:
These are the Powers and Tempers of this Sign.

[V, 504-537; pp. 75-76]

And now Pope's familiar lines on Belinda's toilet.

And now, unveil'd, the *Toilet* stands display'd,
Each Silver Vase in mystic Order laid.
First, rob'd in White, the Nymph intent adores
With Head uncover'd, the *Cosmetic* Pow'rs.
A heav'nly Image in the Glass appears,
To that she bends, to that her Eyes she rears;
Th'inferior Priestess, at her Altar's side,
Trembling, begins the sacred Rites of Pride.
Unnumber'd Treasures ope at once, and here
The various Off'rings of the World appear;
From each she nicely culls with curious Toil,
And decks the Goddess with the glitt'ring Spoil.
This casket *India*'s glowing Gems unlocks,
And all *Arabia* breathes from yonder Box.
The Tortoise here and Elephant unite,
Transform'd to *Combs*, the speckled and the white.
Here Files of Pins extend their shining Rows,
Puffs, Powders, Patches, Bibles, Billet-doux.
Now awful Beauty puts on all its Arms;
The Fair each moment rises in her Charms,

Repairs her Smiles, awakens ev'ry Grace,
And calls forth all the Wonders of her Face;
Sees by Degrees a purer Blush arise,
And keener Lightnings quicken in her Eyes.
The busy *Sylphs* surround their darling Care;
These set the Head, and those divide the Hair,
Some fold the Sleeve, whilst others plait the Gown;
And *Betty*'s prais'd for Labours not her own.

[I, 121-148]

The religious references toward the beginning of Pope's description are paralleled by those in the earlier part of Cassiopeia:

Hence shine our Temples, and our Roman *Jove*
Fills here a Heaven as bright as that above;
Happy this Art employ'd on things Divine,
To frame a Statue, or adorn a Shrine.

Belinda's silver vases stand in mystic order on an altar, where a goddess is served in sacred rites by priestesses; that is, Pope seems to show that the Cassiopeian art which made the vases is "happy" because it is employed to adorn a shrine but at the same time remains "a Slave to pride," for the rites are the "sacred Rites of Pride" (Creech mentions pride again when he writes "they love what decks their Pride"). Pope goes on to write:

Unnumber'd Treasures ope at once, and here
The various Off'rings of the World appear.

There is much about treasures in Cassiopeia, for example, the treasures of Mithridates and Caesar's glorious gems that excel the sun. "The various Off'rings of the World" recalls the mention of the Roman conquests and the search for treasures by land and sea. With this line compare also Creech's "Shines with the Spoils of groaning Provinces" The spoils of the provinces seem to have suggested the offerings of the world, and Pope adapts "shine" and takes over "spoil" for his line "And decks the Goddess with the glitt'ring Spoil" ("deck" is used twice by Creech in this passage). Then *"India*'s glowing Gems" recalls Creech's "Lust for Gems . . . / Which still burns new, and spreads a growing fire."

"Glowing" could have been suggested by "growing." Next note the similarity between "Now Neck, Feet, Hands are deckt" and "Now awful Beauty puts on all its Arms." The listing of the parts of the body in Creech's line could well suggest the arming of an epic hero, like Achilles.

> The silver Cuishes first his Thighs infold;
> Then o'er his Breast was brac'd the hollow Gold.
>
> [*Iliad*, xix, 398].

There is a similarity also between

> The Ornaments of Kings now serve to grace
> A shape, and raise the value of a Face,

and

> Repairs her Smiles, awakens ev'ry Grace,
> And calls forth all the Wonders of her Face.

Trivial though they may be, these resemblances seem to go beyond anything that could reasonably be put down to coincidence; but the full strength of the case only makes itself felt when one considers the comparable position of the two passages in their respective poems, with one standing just before the description of Andromeda, shortly to be quoted, and the other just before what I hope to prove to be Pope's counterpart of that description—and with the break between Cantos I and II of the *Rape of the Lock* corresponding to the transition from one constellation to the other.

The extract from the *Astronomica* which I now quote immediately follows the last.

> Next shines *Andromeda*; she leaves the Sea,
> And on the Right joins *Pisces* twelfth Degree.
> Bright she appears, and gay with sparkling Fires,
> As when young *Perseus* first felt warm desires.
> Unhappy Maid! expos'd to rage Divine,

A faultless Victim for her Mother's Sin:
When Seas let loose o'reflow'd the fruitful Plain,
And Earth now fear'd its ruin from the Main;
Nought could appease, but to the injur'd Flood
The Maid resign'd, to quench its rage with Blood.
This was her Bridal, in her Robes of State;
But not provided for so sad a Fate,
Glorious she lookt, and like the setting Sun,
Greater, tho not so fierce, her Beauty shone.
No joyful Torch its ominous Flames did spread,
No Vows were heard to crown her fruitful Bed;
But Groans and Tears, e're Death pronounc'd her doom
The *Maid* was born alive to her own Tomb.
    Hence fly my Muse, and on the naked Shore
Leave the poor *Maid*, and dare to look no more;
'Twill melt thy Song to turn again to view,
The weeping Parents bid their last adieu;
To see her fetter'd, and expos'd to pain,
Design'd by Nature for another Chain:
To see her hang on Rocks, and by her side
Grim *Death* appear, and point to the swoln Tide.
    Yet turn, and view how she her *Shape* retains,
How *fair* she looks, and *glorious* in her Chains:
With what becoming fear her flowing Vest
Forsakes her Limbs, and leaves her *naked* Breast:
What hidden Beauties are expos'd to sight,
Like *Lightning* glare, but must be lost in night.
By her the *Halcyons* mourn'd, and round the Coast,
That so much Beauty should in vain be lost,
The *Nymphs* repin'd; and *Nereis* from the Deep
Bewail'd her Fate, and did consent to weep:
The gentle *Breeze* that fann'd her golden Locks,
Turn'd into *Sighs*, and murmur'd to the Rocks:
All Nature seem'd concern'd, despairing Grief
Was general, but too weak to yield relief.
Then *Perseus*, glorious with the *Gorgon*'s Spoil,
By *Love* directed to a nobler Toil,
Kind Fortune brought; and at the wondrous sight
He checkt his *Horse*, and stopt his airy flight;
His Hand scarce held his Spoil, *Medusa*'s Eyes
He bore, but now grew stiff at this surprise;

The Chains that held her, and the burth'ned Stone
He *happy* call'd, and *envy'd* joys unknown.
Amaz'd a while he hung, her Form survey'd,
Then heard the Story from the weeping Maid;
Streight in his Breast *high generous* thoughts were bred,
To spoil the *Ocean* to adorn his Bed:
And should a thousand frightful *Gorgons* rise,
He would oppose them for so vast a Prize:
Fixt on these Thoughts he leaves the mournful Shore,
Her Parents chears, and bids them weep no more,
For *Aid* was come: And their Consent desir'd
Was granted soon, and *nobler* warmth inspir'd.
Back he returns: Now teeming Seas did roar,
Waves fled the *Monster*, and o'reflow'd the Shore;
High rais'd his Head, he spouts the Floods around,
All *Nereus* ecchoes, and the Shores resound:
Wide gapes his Mouth, and as on a vast Rock
Dasht on each Tooth the foaming *Billows* broke:
His winding Tail o're half the Main was spread,
The *Ocean* groan'd, Rocks fear'd, and Mountains fled:
     Unhappy Maid! though such an *Aid* was near,
What was thy Mind, and how surpris'd with fear?
How pale thy Look? and how thy Spirit fled
In a deep sigh, and hover'd round thy Head?
How bloodless all thy Limbs, when from deep Caves
The *Monster* rush'd, and bore the foaming Waves
And Fate along? and all design'd for thee
A Prey how little, for so vast a Sea!
     But *Perseus* nimble Aid descends, and hides
The *Gorgon's* Fauchion in his scaly Sides;
He twists upon the Wound, then strives to rear
His head, and shoots up forward thro the Air:
Perseus retires, and still deludes his Foe,
Hangs in the Sky, and aims a surer Blow:
He presses on, and casts his Jaws around,
Bites at the Air, but bites without a Wound.
Then tosses Seas to *Heaven*, spouts purple Floods
At his high Foe, and *drowns* him in the Clouds.
The *Maid* beheld this Fight, and, grateful grown,
Fear'd for his danger, but forgot her own;
Doubtful which way the various Fate inclin'd,

In *Body* less suspended than in *Mind*:
Her doubt not long; for now Success did prove
The great advantage, and the force of Love;
The *Monster* groan'd, and from his Wounds there flow'd
A mighty Stream, and stain'd the Seas with Blood.
Down deep he sinks, but soon he floats again,
And his vast Carcass covers all the Main;
Breathless he lay, yet then his shape did fright;
Tho dead, he was too dreadful for her sight.
Now big with Conquest, from the cleansing Flood
Bright *Perseus* rose, and more August he stood;
Then to the Rocks with eager haste he flies,
Unbinds the Virgin, and enjoys the Prize.
    And hence *Andromeda* now shines a Star,
The Cause, and the Reward of such a War,
As freed the *Ocean*, and restor'd the Main
To *Neptune*'s sway, and fixt him in his Reign.
                              [V, 538-618; pp. 76-79]

Let us look now at the opening of Canto II, where Pope shows us Belinda entering the barge for her trip to Hampton Court. There is strong reason to think the scene is fictional since all the characters in the poem were Roman Catholics and it is unlikely that such a gathering would have been found at Hampton Court. If so, Pope chose the place that most resembled the scene of the story of Andromeda in the *Metamorphoses*, where, as we shall see, there is also a royal palace close to the water. It would have been difficult indeed to adapt the myth to any setting that lacked water.

Not with more Glories, in th' Etherial Plain,
The Sun first rises o'er the purpled Main,
Than issuing forth, the Rival of his Beams
Lanch'd on the Bosom of the Silver *Thames*.
Fair Nymphs, and well-drest Youths around her shone,
But ev'ry Eye was fix'd on her alone.
On her white Breast a sparkling *Cross* she wore,
Which *Jews* might kiss, and Infidels adore.
Her lively Looks a sprightly Mind disclose,
Quick as her Eyes, and as unfix'd as those:

Favours to none, to all she Smiles extends,
Oft she rejects, but never once offends.
Bright as the Sun, her Eyes the Gazers strike,
And, like the Sun, they shine on all alike.
Yet graceful Ease, and Sweetness void of Pride,
Might hide her Faults, if *Belles* had Faults to hide:
If to her share some Female Errors fall,
Look on her Face, and you'll forget 'em all.
       This Nymph, to the Destruction of Mankind,
Nourish'd two Locks, which graceful hung behind
In equal Curls, and well conspir'd to deck
With shining Ringlets the smooth Iv'ry Neck.
Love in these Labyrinths his Slaves detains,
And mighty Hearts are held in slender Chains.
With hairy Sprindges we the Birds betray,
Slight Lines of Hair surprize the Finny Prey,
Fair Tresses Man's Imperial Race insnare,
And Beauty draws us with a single Hair.

                                                    [II, 1-28]

This passage opens with the famous image of the sun (lines 1-4). Andromeda also is compared to the sun,

Glorious she lookt, and like the setting Sun,
Greater, tho not so fierce, her Beauty shone,

but of course the setting sun is not so suitable as the rising sun to mark Belinda's first appearance. Andromeda also is bright, "Bright she appears, and gay with sparkling Fires"; and we may notice that the rhyme words of Pope's first couplet, "Plain" and "Main," occur near at hand in Creech. Pope mentions the sun again a few lines below.

Bright as the Sun, her Eyes the Gazers strike,
And, like the Sun, they shine on all alike.

In the first line he repeats the comparison that in the first edition had appeared less than twenty lines before,

Sol thro' white Curtains did his Beams display,
And op'd those Eyes which brighter shine than they,

and that seems to contain, even in 1712, an echo of Cassiopeia, "The Sun's outshone." Returning to the order of Pope's description, we read,

> Fair Nymphs, and well-drest Youths around her shone,
> But ev'ry Eye was fix'd on her alone,

and we see that Manilius also refers to nymphs surrounding Andromeda:

> By her the *Halcyons* mourn'd, and round the Coast,
> That so much Beauty should in vain be lost,
> The *Nymphs* repin'd.

Andromeda appears as a bride, "This was her Bridal, in her Robes of State," and this, and her isolated position on the rock, suggest that every eye is "fix'd on her alone." Pope continues, "On her white Breast a sparkling *Cross* she wore;" and Manilius refers to Andromeda's breast thus:

>   her flowing Vest
> Forsakes her Limbs, and leaves her *naked* Breast;
> What hidden Beauties are expos'd to sight,
> Like *Lightning* glare.

Though Pope is apparently alluding to Spenser's "on his brest a bloudie Crosse he bore" (*Faerie Queene*, 1, 2, 1), it could be that the sparkling cross also echoes Andromeda's "sparkling fires." Indeed, Belinda's expression, her lively looks and smiles seem to reflect Andromeda's bright and gay appearance as a constellation, as described by Creech, and reverse her tears ("the weeping Maid"), and her "graceful ease" may reflect Andromeda's "becoming fear." Again, Andromeda is called "a faultless Victim," surely a hint for Pope's playful "if *Belles* had Faults to hide."

The first paragraph of Canto II has also, it seems, been influenced by a note of Sandys's on the corresponding place of the *Metamorphoses* where Perseus catches sight of Andromeda and falls in love with her:

> *Perseus* mounting through the ayre, at length arriveth where the faire *Andromeda* was chain'd to a rocke; who [Perseus] at the first sight is enamoured. For certaine subtill rayes expiring from within the heart, where the hottest and sweetest of the vitall blood hath a residence, dart from the eyes of the beautifull, into the eyes of the admiring beholder; and penetrating from thence into the heart, inflames it forthwith with ardent affection; wherein the sudden glances and dartings of the eye are more powerfull then long gazing. [p. 168]

With Sandys's "sudden glances and dartings of the eye," which send out rays, compare Belinda's "quick" and "unfixt" eyes, which are "Bright as the Sun." Long gazing, Sandys tells us, is less powerful than glances, and Belinda is indifferent to the gazers; but between her and the "admiring beholder" (the Baron admires her locks in line 29) love seems to strike, possibly "penetrating into her heart," where Ariel later finds an earthly lover lurking. This borrowing would suggest that Pope is describing love at a glance, rather than flirtatious behaviour on Belinda's part.

Pope then moves on to describe Belinda's locks, and we note that Andromeda's are mentioned by Creech, "The gentle *Breeze* that fanned her golden Locks." The rhyme words in Pope's lines 23–24, "detains" and "Chains," are similar to a pair used by Creech, "retains" and "chains." The decking of Belinda's neck perhaps echoes "Now Neck, Feet, Hands are deckt." We may also note in passing that the reference to the catching of birds and fish is apparently inspired by passages occurring a couple of hundred lines earlier in Creech. Thus compare

> With hairy Sprindges we the Birds betray,
> Slight Lines of Hair surprize the Finny Prey,

with

> They take them flying, or they set their Toyls
> On Boughs or Fields, and catch the Feather'd Spoils.
> Sometimes besiege their Nests with treach'rous Reed,
> [V, 371-372; p. 69]

and with

> Those that are born in every Shore shall lay
> Their Lines and Hooks, and catch the hanging Prey.
>   [V, 396-397; p. 70]

Note the parallel between "betray" and "treacherous," the occurrence of "prey" in Pope and Creech, and how Pope transfers Creech's elegant periphrasis "Feather'd Spoils" from the birds to the fish, where it becomes "Finny Prey."

In each narrative, the hero now enters. In the *Rape of the Lock*, it is the Baron.

> Th' Adventrous *Baron* the bright Locks admir'd,
> He saw, he wish'd, and to the Prize aspir'd:
> Resolv'd to win, he meditates the way,
> By Force to ravish, or by Fraud betray;
> For when Success a Lover's Toil attends,
> Few ask, if Fraud or Force attain'd his Ends.
> For this, ere *Phoebus* rose, he had implor'd
> Propitious Heav'n, and ev'ry Pow'r ador'd,
> But chiefly *Love* — to *Love* an Altar built,
> Of twelve vast *French* Romances, neatly gilt.
> There lay three Garters, half a Pair of Gloves;
> And all the Trophies of his former Loves.
> With tender *Billet-doux* he lights the Pyre,
> And breathes three am'rous Sighs to raise the Fire.
> Then prostrate falls, and begs with ardent Eyes
> Soon to obtain, and long possess the Prize:
> The Pow'rs gave Ear, and granted half his Pray'r,
> The rest, the Winds dispers'd in empty Air.
>   [II, 29-46]

In Manilius it is Perseus.

> Then *Perseus*, glorious with the *Gorgon*'s Spoil,
> By *Love* directed to a nobler Toil,
> Kind Fortune brought; and at the wondrous sight
> He checkt his *Horse*, and stopt his airy flight;
> His Hand scarce held his Spoil, *Medusa*'s Eyes

He bore, but now grew stiff at this surprise;
The Chains that held her, and the burth'ned Stone
He *happy* call'd, and *envy'd* joys unknown.
Amaz'd a while he hung, her Form survey'd,
Then heard the Story from the weeping Maid;
Streight in his Breast *high generous* thoughts were bred,
To spoil the *Ocean* to adorn his Bed:
And should a thousand frightful *Gorgons* rise,
He would oppose them for so vast a Prize:
Fixt on these Thoughts he leaves the mournful Shore,
Her Parents chears, and bids them weep no more,
For *Aid* was come: And their Consent desir'd
Was granted soon, and *nobler* warmth inspir'd.

The parallel here is partly structural. Each extract is in two parts: in the first, each hero sees the object that he desires and he resolves to obtain it; in the second, he seeks the agreement of another party — the God of Love, Andromeda's parents — to his success. There are also some detailed echoes of Manilius and Ovid. Andromeda is a "prize," and Pope says the Baron "to the Prize aspir'd." Perseus contemplates force,

>   And should a thousand frightful *Gorgons* rise,
>   He would oppose them for so vast a Prize;

and the Baron meditates "By Force to ravish." The line "For when success a Lover's Toil attends" recalls Creech's "By *Love* directed to a nobler Toil." The next line, "Few ask, if Force or Fraud attain'd his Ends," contains the same question as Cepheus has when he asks Perseus in the *Metamorphoses* at the feast after the death of the monster:

>   Now tell, O valiant Knight,
>   By what felicitie of force or sleight,
>   You got this purchase of the snaky haires.
>   [IV, 770-771; Sandys's translation, pp. 150-151]

(There is an imitation of this in Canto II, line 103, also, "Some dire Disaster, or by Force, or Slight," where "dire disaster" reverses "felicitie.") There is little difference between an adventur-

ous baron and a valiant knight, especially when the feat of both is to capture hairs.

There is another echo of Ovid in

> For this, ere *Phoebus* rose, he had implor'd
> Propitious Heav'n, and ev'ry Pow'r ador'd,

for Perseus had told Andromeda's parents,

> I'le trie (so favour me the Powres divine)
> That shee, sav'd by my valour, may be mine.
>> [IV, 702-703; p. 149]

"Propitious" is probably an adaptation of Sandys's "so favour me." In Ovid, also, Perseus builds altars and sacrifices, but after his victory; he had no time to do so before.

Pope now gives us the description of Belinda in the barge.

> But now secure the painted Vessel glides,
> The Sun-beams trembling on the floating Tydes,
> While melting Musick steals upon the Sky,
> And soften'd Sounds along the Waters die.
> Smooth flow the Waves, the Zephyrs gently play,
> *Belinda* smil'd, and all the World was gay.
> All but the *Sylph* — With careful Thoughts opprest
> Th'impending Woe sate heavy on his Breast.
>> [II, 47-54]

This passage reverses Manilius's description of the appearance of the monster, for which the barge is a substitute (Ovid had compared it to a vessel, "a Gally with fore-fixed Prow"). Here are Creech's lines:

> Waves fled the *Monster*, and o'reflow'd the Shore;
> High rais'd his Head, he spouts the Floods around,
> All *Nereus* ecchoes, and the Shores resound:
> Wide gapes his Mouth, and as on a vast Rock
> Dasht on each Tooth the foaming *Billows* broke:

His winding Tail o're half the Main was spread,
The *Ocean* groan'd, Rocks fear'd, and Mountains fled:
   Unhappy Maid! though such an *Aid* was near,
What was thy Mind, and how surpris'd with fear?
How pale thy Look? And how thy Spirit fled
In a deep sigh, and hover'd round thy Head?

Pope's description is almost a line-by-line softening of this extract. Contrast

But now secure the painted Vessel glides,
The Sun-beams trembling on the floating Tydes,

with

   Now teeming Seas did roar,
Waves fled the *Monster*, and o'reflow'd the Shore;

and

While melting Musick steals upon the Sky,
And soften'd Sounds along the Waters die,

with "All *Nereus* ecchoes, and the Shores resound" and "Smooth flow'd the Waves" with

   as on a vast Rock
Dasht on each Tooth the foaming *Billows* broke.

"Belinda smil'd" reverses the description of Andromeda's appearance ("How pale thy Look") and "and all the World was gay" goes back to and reverses Creech's words "All Nature seem'd concern'd." It seems probable also that Pope's mention of Ariel,

All but the *Sylph* — With careful Thoughts opprest,
Th' impending Woe sate heavy on his Breast,

was suggested by Creech's

   how thy Spirit fled
In a deep sigh, and hover'd round thy Head?

Ariel is, in another sense, Belinda's spirit and would have sighed at Belinda's "impending woe."

After a considerable gap, mainly occupied by sylphs, we return to Andromeda with the game of ombre whose decisive moment is drawn from the slaying of the monster:

> At this, the Blood the Virgin's Cheek forsook,
> A livid Paleness spreads o'er all her Look;
> She sees, and trembles at th' approaching Ill,
> Just in the Jaws of Ruin, and *Codille.*
> And now, (as oft in some distemper'd State)
> On one nice *Trick* depends the gen'ral Fate.
> An *Ace* of Hearts steps forth: The *King* unseen
> Lurk'd in her Hand, and mourn'd his captive *Queen.*
> He springs to Vengeance with an eager pace,
> And falls like Thunder on the prostrate *Ace.*
> The Nymph exulting fills with Shouts the Sky,
> The Walls, the Woods, and long Canals reply.
>
> [III, 89-100]

Compare this with

> Unhappy Maid! though such an *Aid* was near,
> What was thy Mind, and how surpris'd with fear?
> How pale thy Look?
> . . . .
> How bloodless all thy Limbs, when from deep Caves,
> The *Monster* rush'd, and bore the foaming Waves
> And Fate along?
> . . . .
> But *Perseus* nimble Aid descends, and hides
> The *Gorgon's* Fauchion in his scaly Sides.

Creech's phrases "How bloodless all thy Limbs" and "How pale thy Look" have been taken over and slightly adapted. Creech's "Maid" becomes "Virgin" (Manilius has *virgo*), and his "how surpris'd with fear" becomes "she trembles." The monster rushing from the caves is, without doubt, an "approaching ill"; and the "Jaws of Ruin" recall "casts his Jaws around" and "Wide gapes his Mouth." Perseus's "nimble aid" has been adapted to

"He springs to Vengeance with an eager pace," and the last couplet quoted from Pope is an expansion of a line of Sandys's from exactly the same point in the narrative "The shore rings with th' applause that fills the sky" (IV, 735; p. 150).

In the *Metamorphoses* Perseus then sacrifices and a banquet follows. Here is the passage from Sandys:

> The sacred Fires with rich perfumes are fed;
> The house hung round with Garlands; every-where
> Melodious Harps and Songs salute the eare;
> Of jocond mirth the free and happy signes:
> With Dores display'd, the golden Palace shines.
> The *Cephen* Nobles, and each stranger Guest,
> Together enter to this sumptuous Feast.
> The Banquet done, with generous wines they cheare
> Their hightned spirits: *Perseus* longs to heare
> Their fashions, manners, and originall;
> Who, by *Lyncides* is inform'd of all.
>
> [IV, 759-767; p. 150]

Compare with this the opening of Canto III.

> Close by those Meads for ever crown'd with Flow'rs,
> Where *Thames* with Pride surveys his rising Tow'rs,
> There stands a Structure of Majestick Frame.
> . . . .
> Hither the Heroes and the Nymphs resort,
> To taste awhile the Pleasures of a Court;
> In various Talk th' instructive hours they past,
> Who gave the *Ball*, or paid the *Visit* last.
>
> [III, 1-3, 9-12]

Then, after the description of the talk, there is a long interval; but in the first edition there were only six lines before Pope continued with the coffee drinking:

> For lo! the Board with Cups and Spoons is crown'd,
> The Berries crackle, and the Mill turns round.
> On shining Altars of *Japan* they raise

The silver Lamp; the fiery Spirits blaze.
From silver Spouts the grateful Liquors glide,
While *China*'s Earth receives the smoking Tyde.
At once they gratify their Sense and Taste,
And frequent Cups prolong the rich Repast.
                                        [III, 105-112]

The parallel between Pope and Ovid is clear. In each there is a
palace, which the company enters for refreshment and gossipy
talk in a festive atmosphere. The parallel extends to details and
phrases; for example, the palace in Ovid is hung with garlands
while the Hampton meadows are crowned with flowers; in Ovid,
"they" cheer their heightened spirits while in Pope they gratify
their sense and taste; and "rich Repast" in Pope is a paraphrase of
"sumptuous feast."

Pope describes the rape of the lock itself as follows:

He takes the Gift with rev'rence, and extends
The little Engine on his Fingers' Ends,
This just behind *Belinda*'s Neck he spread,
As o'er the fragrant Steams she bends her Head.
. . . .
    The Peer now spreads the glittering *Forfex* wide,
T'inclose the Lock; now joins it, to divide.
Ev'n then, before the fatal Engine clos'd,
A wretched *Sylph* too fondly interpos'd;
Fate urg'd the Sheers, and cut the *Sylph* in twain,
(But Airy Substance soon unites again)
The meeting Points the sacred Hair dissever
From the fair Head, for ever and for ever!
    Then flash'd the living Lightning from her Eyes,
And Screams of Horror rend th' affrighted Skies.
                                        [III, 131-134, 147-156]

This scene of violence corresponds to the slaying of the monster
described in the *Metamorphoses* as follows:

So swiftly stoops high-pitcht *Inachides*
Through singing ayre: then on his backe doth seaze:

And neere his right fin sheaths his crooked sword
Up to the hilts; who deeply wounded, roar'd.
                              [IV, 718-721; Sandys's translation, p. 149]

Naturally enough, there is little verbal echo. The harmless bisection of the sylph recalls, perhaps, Manilius's "bites without a wound," and the screams of horror rending the sky may be another, fainter reminiscence of "The shore rings with th' applause that fills the sky."

The Baron now gives expression to his triumph in the following lines:

Let Wreaths of Triumph now my Temples twine,
(The Victor cry'd) the glorious Prize is mine!
While Fish in Streams, or Birds delight in Air,
. . . .
So long my Honour, Name, and Praise shall live!
                              [III, 161-3, 170]

Manilius describes Perseus in the following:

Now big with Conquest, from the cleansing Flood
Bright *Perseus* rose, and more August he stood;
Then to the Rocks with eager haste he flies,
Unbinds the Virgin, and enjoys the Prize.

There are verbal parallels here. Perseus "enjoys the Prize"; the Baron says, "The . . . Prize is mine." Perseus is "more August"; the Baron has gained "Honour, Name, and Praise."

We now pass to the beginning of Canto IV, where we see Belinda in a state of rising anger over the loss of her hair. Then follow Umbriel's visit to the Cave of Spleen and his return with a bag and a vial which further worsen female tempers. Thalestris makes a fierce speech, Sir Plume attempts to bring peace, the Baron refuses it, and Belinda mourns her lock. Canto V begins with Clarissa's vain call to good humour, and a brawl ensues between the men and the women. The women are on the point of

winning, but the lock has disappeared; in fact, it has become a star, and the poem ends.

With further changes in the scheme of substitution, these events (except the visit to the Cave of Spleen) parallel those that interrupt the victory banquet at the beginning of Book V of the *Metamorphoses*. Belinda now corresponds to Phineus, who is Andromeda's uncle and also her betrothed, and who rushes into the hall in a rage. Cepheus attempts to calm him, but he attacks Perseus and starts a fight in which many are killed. Here are Sandys's lines:

> Whil'st the *Danaean* Heroe this relates,
> Amidst th' assembly of the *Cephen* States;
> Exalted voyces through the Palace ring:
> Not like to theirs who at a marriage sing;
> But such as menace warre. The Nuptiall Feast,
> Thus turn'd to tumult, to the life exprest
> A peaceful Sea, whose brow no frowne deformes,
> Streight ruffled into billowes by rude stormes.
> First *Phineus*, the rash Author of this warre,
> Shaking a Launce, began the deadly jarre.
> Lo, I the man, that will upon thy life
> Revenge, said he, the rapture of my wife.
> Nor shall thy wings, nor *Jove* in forged gold,
> Work thy escape. About to throwe: O hold!
> Perplexed *Cepheus* cries: What wilt thou do?
> What furie, frantick brother, tempts thee to
> So foule a fact? Is this the recompence
> For such high merit? For her life's defence?
> Not *Perseus*, but th'incens't *Nereides*,
> But horned *Hammon*, and the wrath of Seas
> (That Orke that sought my bowels to devoure)
> Hath snatcht her from thee; ravisht in the houre
> Of her exposure. But thy crueltie
> Perhaps was well content that she should die,
> To ease thy losse with ours. May't not suffice,
> That she was bound in chaines before thine eyes;
> That thou, her Uncle, and her Husband, brought
> Her perill no prevention, nor none sought;

But that anothers aid thou must envy,
And claime the Trophys of his victory?
. . . .
    He, without answere, rowling to and fro
His eyes on either, doubts at which to throwe:
And pausing, his ill-aymed lance at length
At *Perseus* hurles, with rage-redoubled strength.
                    [V, 1-25, 30-33; pp. 171-172]

Here, as in the *Rape of the Lock*, a scene of peaceful refreshment is suddenly turned into one of conflict and revenge.[1] The
counterpart of Cepheus's speech of attempted conciliation is not
Clarissa's (which was not, of course, added until 1717), but Thalestris's; but it is a reversed counterpart, for while Phineus could
not be restrained, Belinda had to be urged to battle. For verbal
similarities, notice the occurrence of "ravish" and cognate words
in Sandys and Pope (10, 103) and compare the rhetorical questions near the beginning of each speech:

            Is this the recompence
    For such high merit? For her life's defence?

and

    Was it for this you took such constant Care
    The *Bodkin*, *Comb*, and *Essence* to prepare;
    For this your Locks in Paper-Durance bound,
    For this with tort'ring Irons wreath'd around?
                    [IV, 97-100]

The latter couplet appears to echo the reference to Andromeda
"bound in chains before thine eyes". Thalestris's "wretched
Maid" seems to echo Creech's "unhappy Maid."

In the fight itself, one or two Ovidian details have been taken
over. Dapperwit dies in song, as does the minstrel Lampetides
who had been invited to sing at the banquet:

    concidit et digitis morientibus ille retemptat
    fila lyrae, casuque fuit miserabile carmen,
                    [V, 117-118]

or

> His dying fingers warble in his fall:
> And then, by chance, the Song was tragicall.
> > [Sandys's translation, p. 174]

The Baron's "dying" words,

> Nor think, to die dejects my lofty Mind;
> All that I dread, is leaving you behind!
> Rather than so, ah let me still survive,
> And burn in *Cupid*'s Flames, — but burn alive,
> > [V, 99-102]

recall two of the deaths in Ovid. First, that of Lycabas, who is
reconciled to dying by the thought that he is not leaving behind
his beloved Atys, who has just been killed.

> Then chearfully expires his parting breath:
> Rejoycing to be joyn'd to him in death.
> > [V, 73; Sandys's translation, p. 173]

Then, the death of Emathion, whose head, having been struck off,
rolls onto an altar and briefly burns alive in the god's flames:

> *Cromis*, as he imbrac't the Altar, lopt
> His shaking head; which on the Altar dropt:
> Whose halfe-dead tongue yet curses; and expires
> His righteous soule amidst the sacred Fires.
> > [V, 103-106; Sandys's translation, p. 173]

The final event in the *Rape of the Lock* is the Lock's becoming a star,

> But trust the Muse — she saw it upward rise,
> Tho' mark'd by none but quick Poetic Eyes:
> . . . .
> A sudden Star, it shot thro' liquid Air,
> And drew behind a radiant *Trail of Hair*.
> > [V, 123-124, 127-128]

The same, as we know, happened to Andromeda at the end of Manilius's narrative: "And hence *Andromeda* now shines a Star." Pope is undoubtedly also thinking of Ovid's last metamorphosis, that of the soul of Julius Caesar:

> luna volat altius illa
> flammiferumque trahens spatioso vertice crinem
> stella micat. . . .
>   [XV, 848-850; see the note in the Twickenham edition]

or

> When once let loose, It forth-with upward flew,
> And after it long blazing tresses drew.
>   [XV, 848-849; Sandys's translation, p. 509]

Belinda is to find consolation for the loss of her lock in its translation to the sky, as Rome did for loss of her greatest soul apart from Augustus.[2]

The case rests on this evidence. Although a few of the verbal resemblances may be fortuitous, there are enough that cannot be to establish the connection between the claimed sources and Pope's poem. It is interesting to note also how the Andromeda legend, especially as recounted in the *Astronomica*, communicates an air of tension and apprehension to Pope's earlier cantos, while the battle scene at the beginning of Ovid's fifth book illustrates, equally to Pope's purpose, the destructive power of insensate intemperance. One would not, however, claim that acquaintance with this source adds anything important to our understanding of the *Rape of the Lock*; still less, it is hardly necessary to add, could one claim that it calls in question Pope's originality or Johnson's judgment in his *Life of Pope* that "he had *Invention*, by which new trains of thought are formed, and new scenes of imagery are displayed, as in the *Rape of the Lock*." Anyone who thinks differently may like to try to concoct a poem from some other of the stories in the *Metamorphoses*; there are about two hundred and fifty. The chief interest lies, perhaps, in what we learn about Pope's methods. In the *Imitations of Horace*, as we know, he practised adaptation on a large scale, but here we

find him composing in much the same way some twenty years earlier. One great difference, of course, is that with the *Rape of the Lock* the source adds nothing to the poem, whereas the *Imitations of Horace* cannot have its fullest effect unless it is read with the Latin printed opposite, as Pope wished. The chapters that follow attempt to trace borrowings which can truly illuminate the poems in which they occur but which up until now have remained hidden.

CHAPTER 3

The Wild Heap and the Ordered Frame

I

Let us turn now to examine Pope's treatment of a single theme, that of the Creation. It is a cosmological theme, and recent critics have indeed paid much attention to the cosmological aspects of his work, particularly to the doctrine that seemingly conflicting forces in the universe are reconciled into an ordered whole.

> Not *Chaos*-like together crush'd and bruis'd,
> But as the World, harmoniously confus'd:
> Where Order in Variety we see,
> And where, tho' all things differ, all agree.
> [Windsor Forest, 13-16]

The meaning of these lines from *Windsor Forest* and of the passage in which they are set has been recovered after apparently having been lost for generations, and we now understand that the lines present not merely a landscape painting but a symbolic account of the Forest as a microcosm of the universe. Earl Wasserman has shown in *The Subtler Language* that *Windsor Forest*, as a whole and in all its details, is a cosmological poem embodying the principle of *concordia discors* which "permeates almost all of Pope's writings." Even when discussing not overtly cosmological passages, critics tend to use cosmological language in reflection of his thought. Yet much as has already been done to study Pope as a

33

poet of cosmic order, the study can be further extended by tracing his borrowings from certain passages of ancient cosmological poetry and other sources that he continually used as the inspiration and vehicle of his own cosmological doctrine. He was not indeed the first to use them, but what with earlier poets usually had been occasional and local with him was systematic and pervasive.

The most important by far of Pope's cosmological sources is the remarkable account of the Creation of the beginning of the *Metamorphoses*, which seems to have become perhaps the most influential document of *concordia discors*. Pope refers to the original and to Sandys about equally, and occasionally glances also at Dryden's freer and more flowing translation. The original and Dryden's translation are easily available, and the reader of this chapter will find it useful to have them at hand. Sandys's translation follows:

> Of bodies chang'd to other shapes I sing.
> Assist, you Gods (from you these changes spring)
> And, from the Worlds first fabrick to these times,
> Deduce my never-discontinued Rymes.
>   The Sea, the Earth, all-covering Heaven unfram'd,
> One face had Nature, which they *Chaos* nam'd:
> An undigested lump; a barren load,
> Where jarring seeds of things ill-joyn'd aboad.
> No *Titan* yet the world with light adornes;
> Nor waxing *Phoebe* fill'd her wained hornes:
> Nor hung the selfe-poiz'd Earth in thin Ayre plac'd;
> Nor *Amphitrite* the vast shore imbrac'd.
> With Earth, was Ayre and Sea: the Earth unstable,
> The Ayre was darke, the Sea un-navigable:
> No certain forme to any one assign'd:
> This, that resists. For, in one body joyn'd,
> The Cold and Hot, the Drie and Humid fight;
> The Soft and Hard, the Heavie with the Light.
> But God, the better Nature, this decides:
> Who Earth from Heaven, the Sea from Earth divides:
> And purer Heaven extracts from grosser Ayre.
> All which unfolded by his prudent care
> From that blinde Masse; the happily dis-joyn'd
> With strifelesse peace He to their seats confin'd.

Forth-with up-sprung the quick and waightlesse Fire,
Whose flames unto the highest Arch aspire:
The next, in levitie and place, is Ayre:
Grosse Elements to thicker Earth repayre
Selfe-clog'd with waight: the Waters flowing round,
Possesse the last, and solid *Tellus* bound.
    What God soever this division wrought,
And every part to due proportion brought;
First, least the Earth unequall should appeare,
He turn'd it round, in figure of a Spheare;
Then, Seas diffus'd; commanding them to roare
With ruffling Winds, and give the Land a shore.
To those he addeth Springs, Ponds, Lakes immense;
And Rivers, whom their winding borders fence:
Of these, not few Earth's thirsty jawes devoure;
The rest, their streams into the Ocean poure;
When, in that liquid Plaine, with freer wave,
The foamie Cliffes, in stead of Banks, they lave:
Bids Trees increase to Woods, the Plaines extend,
The rocky Mountaynes rise, and Vales descend.
    Two equall Zones, on either side, dispose
The measur'd Heavens; a fifth, more hot then those.
As many Lines th' included Globe divide:
I' th' midst unsufferable beams reside;
Snow clothes the other two: the temperate hold
'Twixt these their seats, the Heat well mixt with Cold.
    As Earth, as Water, upper Ayre out-waighs;
So much doth Ayre Fire's lighter balance raise.
There, He commands the changing Clouds to stray;
There, thundering terrors mortall mindes dismay;
And with the Lightning, Winds ingendring Snow:
Yet not permitted every way to blow;
Who hardly now to teare the Worlde refraine
(So Brothers jarre!) though they divided raigne,
To *Persis* and *Sabbaea*, *Eurus* flies;
Whose gums perfume the blushing Mornes up-rise:
Next to the Evening, and the Coast that glowes
With setting *Phoebus*, flowrie *Zeph'rus* blowes:
In *Scythia* horrid *Boreas* holds his raigne,
Beneath *Boötes* and the frozen Waine:
The Land to this oppos'd, doth *Auster* steepe
With fruitfull showres, and clouds which ever weepe.

Above all these he plac't the liquid Skies;
Which, void of earthly dregs, did highest rise.
    Scarce had He all thus orderly dispos'd;
When as the Starres their radiant heads disclos'd
(Long hid in Night) and shone through all the skie.
Then, that no place should unpossessed lie,
Bright Constellations, and faire figured Gods,
In heavenly Mansions fixt their blest abodes:
The glittering Fishes to the Flouds repayre;
The Beasts to Earth, the Birds resort to Ayre.
    The nobler Creature, with a minde possesst,
Was wanting yet, that should command the rest.
That Maker, the best World's originall,
Either him fram'd of seed Cælestiall;
Or Earth, which late he did from Heaven divide,
Some sacred seeds retain'd, to Heaven ally'd:
Which with the living streame *Prometheus* mixt;
And in that artificiall structure fixt
The forme of all th'all ruling Deities.
And whereas others see with downe-cast eyes,
He with a loftie looke did Man indue,
And bade him heavens transcendent glories view.
So, that rude Clay, which had no forme afore,
Thus chang'd, of Man the unknowne figure bore.

                          [I, 1-88; pp. 1-3]

Ovid here sets out ideas that were already commonplace in his own time and were to remain in the European mind until Pope's generation. Sandys's note would have provided Pope with a commentary. It is long, but part of it may be quoted:

Then hee proceeds to the description of that confused Masse, which the Platonists call the undigested World, as the World the digested *Chaos*: ordered, as they say by Love; who raised the heavy, illuminated the obscure, quickned the dead, gave forme to the deformed, and perfection to the imperfect: which was no other than that harmony in Nature created by the Almighties *Fiat*. And although by not expressing the originall he seemes to intimate the eternitie of his *Chaos*: yet appeares in the rest so consonant to the truth, as doubtlesse he had either seene the Books of *Moses*, or receaved that doctrine by tradition. He confesseth God, not disguiz-

ing his name . . . to be the Creator of the World and maker of all things: and by that word *Commanded*, so often reiterated, that hee made them by his Word only. Whom he also calleth the *Better Nature*; so named by the Stoicke: *Wilt thou call him Nature? Thou offendest not: it is he by whose spirit wee live, of whom all things were borne.* The better concludes a worse, which was *Chaos*: God they held to be the Minde, and *Chaos* the Matter: the Minde called by *Plato* the worlds Architectresse. [p. 19]

The following lines in which Manilius briefly rehearses six ancient theories of the origin of the universe (and which, incidentally, Dryden imitates in *Religio Laici*), should also be read with the passage from Ovid:

> But now since *Fate* and *Verse* do joyntly flow
> From *Heaven*, and both rule equally below,
> First let my *Muse* whole Nature's Face design,
> Its Figure draw, and finish every Line.
> Whether from *Seed* it ne'er began to be,
> Secure from *Fate*, and from *Corruption* free;
> Knew no *Beginning*, and no *Ending* fears,
> But was, and will be, as it now appears.
> Or huddled *Chaos* by a wondrous Birth
> Archt the vast Sky and fixt the solid Earth;
> And when this shining World once rais'd its Head
> To Shades *Infernal* banisht *Darkness* fled.
> Or whether unseen *Atoms* blindly thrown
> Compos'd it, and as Years whirle nimbly on,
> It must dissolve, and as it first was wrought
> From almost Nothing, fall to almost Nought.
> Or rose from working Fire's enlivening Rays,
> Which form Heaven's Eyes, and live in every Mass,
> In *Thunder* roar, and in the *Lightning* blaze.
> Or whether *Water* which combines the Frame
> Compos'd, and keeps it from the loosning Flame.
> Or whether Water, Air, and Flame and Earth
> Know no beginning, no *first* seeds of Birth;
> But first in Being from themselves arose,
> And as four Members the vast *God* compose;
> In which Thin, Thick, Hot, Cold, and Moist and Dry,
> For mutual Actions mutual parts supply.

From whose agreeing disagreement springs
The numerous odd Variety of Things.
These qualities to act provoke the Seed,
Make *Vital* Elements and Bodies breed.
    What 'twas at first, and whence the *All* began
Is doubted, and the Doubt too deep for Man;
And let it be, but whencesoe'er it came
Its Face is certain, 'tis an *order'd* Frame.

[I, 118-148; pp. 7-8]

Creech, following Sherburne, attributes these six cosmogonies to Xenophanes, the Phoenicians, Epicurus, Heraclitus, Thales, and Empedocles respectively. We can see that Ovid's Creation is a blend chiefly of the "Phoenician" story of the original Chaos and the "Empedoclean" theory of the four elements. Pope's view of the former is probably best represented by Creech's note.

> This blind fancy we owe to the Phoenicians, who (if *Philo Biblius's Sancuniathon* may be trusted) taught that the Principles of the Universe were a Spirit of dark Air, and a confus'd Chaos; this Spirit at last began to Love, and joyning with the Chaos, produced [*Mɔt*] or slime, and thence fashioned the World. And hence likely the more sober part of the Greek Philosophers, (for they were but borrowers of Learning) who requir'd two eternal principles, the one *active* and the other *passive*, such as *Plato, Anaxagoras, etc.* took their notions, and having added some few new ornaments, vented them for their own. [p. 38]

It was the "Phoenician" ingredient that was commonly held to account for the striking resemblances between Ovid and Genesis which had long preoccupied commentators. Grotius, for example, in his *De Veritate Religionis Christianae* held that the Phoenicians had carried the books of Moses from the Hebrews to the Greeks and that the Creation story contained in the surviving fragments of Sanchuniathon (supposedly a Phoenician living before the Trojan War, about whom a book by Bishop Richard Cumberland was published in 1720) show them in transmission. Sandys, as we have seen, agrees that Ovid must have seen them or otherwise have received their tradition; Sherburne also follows Grotius.

Pope would have connected the so-called Phoenician doctrine with other thinkers, such as Anaxagoras, who, according to Stanley, taught that "when all things were at first confusedly mingled together, [the divine Mind] came and reduced them to order" (p. 63). He would also, of course, have recognized the "Empedoclean" doctrine of the strife (*neikos*) of the opposites and the elements, ordered by love (*philotēs*) into *concordia discors* (or "discordia concors," as Manilius calls it). Stanley's account of Empedocles, and of love and strife, is particularly important for us.

> He held that there are four Elements, Fire, Air, Water, Earth; and two principal powers, Amity and Discord; one unitive, the other discretive. . . . These are in an incessant mutation, whereby there is such an eternal production of things. . . . Before the four Elements, there are certain less fragments, as it were Elements of Elements, of similar parts, and round. . . . Nature is nothing but the mixture and separation of the Elements. [pp. 432-433]

In a note on page 13 of his translation, explaining the lines of Manilius just quoted, Sherburne shows us the doctrine at a later stage of its development:

> To this purpose *Lactantius, l.2. Philosophi quidam et poetae discordi Concordia Mundum constare dixerunt*, i.e. some Philosophers and Poets report the World to consist of discording Concord: so likewise *Cassiodorus* (*lib. 2. Variarum*) *Merito dicunt Philosophi Elementa sibi Mutuis complexibus illigari et mirabili conjungi foederatione, quae inter se contraria intelliguntur varietate pugnare*. [The philosophers well say that the elements, which are thought to fight each other in their contrary nature, are bound by mutual embraces and joined in a marvelous alliance.] This dissonant Harmony of Nature being represented by *Orpheus* in his *Tetrachord*; In which, as there were four strings, from the mixture of whose different Tones resulted a sweet Harmony; so by concourse and mixture of the four Elements, all things are generated. And as in the Tetrachord the [hupatē hupatōn] rendred the gravest sound, [Nētē] the most acute, and the nearest in gravity of sound to the first came the [parhupatē hupatōn], to the second in acuteness the [paranētē]: So among the Elements, there is one of the heaviest,

Earth, and one the lightest, Fire, answering to the two first Notes;
Water and Air answering to the two intermediate Tones. This admirable consent of the contrary Elements is here [i.e. in Sherburne's translation] not unaptly called *The Matrimonial Band of
Nature*. And for this reason, saies *Lactantius* (*loco citato*) The Marriages of the Antients were confirmed and plighted by the Sacrament of two contrary Elements, Fire and Water. In regard that Heat
and Moisture are the Parents of all Generation, as *Ovid* (*l.*1
Metam.) hath likewise exprest it.

> *Quippe ubi Temperiem sumpsere Humorque Calorque,*
> *Concipiunt, et ab his oriuntur cuncta duobus,*
> *Cumque sit Ignis Aquae Pugnax, vapor humidus omnes*
> *Res Creat; et* Discors Concordia *foetibus apta est.*

[For, Heat and Moysture, when they temperate grow,
Forth-with conceive; and life on things bestow.
From striving Fire and Water all proceede;
Discording Concord ever apt to breede.
                    (I, 429-432; Sandys's translation, p. 10)]

This philosophy of *concordia discors* (a phrase seemingly
invented by Horace to apply to Empedocles) permeates Ovid's
Creation. Originally the opposites and the elements were "ill-
joined" in a *rudis indigestaque moles*, or a "heap of jarring
atoms," a state utterly unlike the world we know. However, God
and an improved Nature composed their strife by separating them
and by arranging them to form the universe. Ovid's description of
the globe dwells throughout on their interaction, for example, in
the interlocking pattern of earth and water. A winding river is a
perfect symbol of the harmonious interaction of elements. The
motion and fluidity of the water are continually checked and
turned by the stability and solidity of the earth, so that the river
can only make its way where the earth permits it; yet it does, in the
end, make its way, at once irrigating and draining the earth, a
source of life and beauty. A third element, air, acts on the waters.
The temperate zones are the product of the blending of hot and
cold, and the discord of the winds is tempered by separation and
arrangement. Then, as soon as the necessary order has been

achieved, light shines and life begins in every element. It will be
remembered (Stephanus makes it clear) that *kosmos* means, in its
primary sense, "order," and the meaning "world" is derived from
that sense; thus the creation of order and the creation of the world
are the same.

The Creation passage is surely a key to the *Metamorphoses*
not merely because the ordering of Chaos was the first and greatest
of metamorphoses but because the "Empedoclean" cosmology is
perfectly suited to the linking theme of change. As Pythagoras
explains in his discourse in the last book, the elements that compose the world themselves change continuously.

> All things are mix'd of these, which all contain,
> And into these are all resolv'd again.
> Earth rarifies to Dew, expanded more
> The subtil Dew in Air begins to soar;
> Spreads as she flies, and weary of her Name
> Extenuates still, and changes into Flame,

And then down the scale to earth again, so that

> Thus are their Figures never at a stand,
> But chang'd by Nature's innovating Hand;
> All Things are alter'd.
> [XV 245-248 and 252-253; Dryden's translation, 374-379 and 386-388]

Furthermore, in his lines on the creation of Man, Ovid shows us
how our bodies and souls are composed of the same four elements,
so that we too must be driven by strife and love and must be subject
to the same law of mutability, as again Pythagoras explains:

> And therefore I conclude, whatever lies
> In Earth, or flits in Air, or fills the Skies,
> All suffer change, and we, that are of Soul
> And Body mix'd, are Members of the whole.
> [XV, 454-456; Dryden's translation, 670-673]

Within this cosmological setting, the metamorphoses of

Ovid's poem are not merely contingent common features of his stories but particular manifestations of a universal law, arising of necessity from the nature of the world. In consequence, they give the poem, which, with its continual changes of narrative, seems to obey the same law and imitate the world in its form, a kind of unity of action, and perhaps bring it within the spirit of Aristotle's dictum that poetry is more philosophical and serious than history because it deals with generalities and history with particulars. The *Metamorphoses* must therefore be taken as being, among other things, a cosmological poem. This was well understood by Sandys as he shows in his prefatory *Minde of the Frontispeece and Argument of this Worke*, which begins.

> FIRE, AIRE, EARTH, WATER, all the Opposites
> That strove in *Chaos*, powrefull LOVE unites;
> And from their Discord drew this Harmonie,
> Which smiles in *Nature*: who, with ravisht eye,
> Affects his owne-made *Beauties*. But, our *Will*,
> *Desire*, and *Powres Irascible*, the skill
> Of PALLAS orders; who the *Mind* attires
> With all *Heroick Vertues*: This aspires
> To *Fame* and *Glorie*; by her noble Guide
> Eternized, and well-nigh Deifi'd.
> But who forsake that faire *Intelligence*,
> To follow *Passion*, and voluptuous *Sense*;
> That shun the Path and Toyles of HERCULES;
> Such, charm'd by CIRCE's luxurie, and ease,
> Themselves deforme: 'twixt whom, so great an ods;
> That these are held for Beasts, and those for Gods.

The second line alludes to strife and love, the third to *concordia discors*.

Ovid writes, then, as a poet, rather than as a philosopher; his account of Creation is merely a story, without evidence or reasoning to support it. Nevertheless, it is lucid and highly organized, with every detail illustrating the idea of elemental concord replacing strife. Standing as it does at the beginning of one of the best known of all poems, it probably played no small part in ensuring

the prevalence of the idea of *concordia discors*; and whether this is so or not, there is no doubt that it had much to offer as a model. It was broadly acceptable to orthodoxy as containing as much of the truth revealed to Moses as could be hoped for in a pagan text of 8 A.D., and it bears also a certain resemblance to the great panorama of an ordered universe in Psalm 104; but since it presented the Creation more as an act of art and intellect than, like Genesis, of majesty and will, it was more amenable to use as an allegory for various human endeavors. With its large admixture of the pre-Aristotelian philosophical tradition, which had flowered again in the Renaissance, it was in tune with modern thought. Allusions to it would readily be recognized, and for writers of heroic couplets there was the added advantage that fragments of Sandys could easily be incorporated into their work.

Ovid is not a polemicist; nevertheless, when he attributes the Creation of the universe to God's mind and power of design, he takes the side of the Stoics in the great cosmological controversy of the ancient world. The opposite doctrine, that held by the Epicureans, was that the order of the universe had arisen, not by God's decree ("fate") or design or by any operation of mind, but by mere chance from a chaotic swirl of atoms and might at any time be destroyed again by chance. Cicero had made the controversy the subject of his philosophical dialogue *De Natura Deorum*, and in poetry Lucretius had argued the Epicurean case, which Manilius attacked in the following lines.

> A most convincing Reason drawn from Sense,
> That this vast Frame is mov'd by *Providence*,
> Which like the Soul doth every Whirl advance;
> It must be *God*, nor was it made by *Chance*;
> As *Epicurus* dreamt, He madly thought
> This beauteous Frame of heedless *Atoms* wrought,
> That Seas and Earth, the Stars and spacious Air
> Which forms New Worlds, or doth the Old repair,
> First rose from these, and still supply'd remain,
> And All must be, when Chance shall break the Chain,
> Dissolv'd to these wild *Principles* again.
> Absurd and Nonsense! *Atheist* use thine Eyes,

And having view'd the order of the Skies,
Think, if Thou canst, that Matter blindly hurld,
Without a Guide should frame this wondrous World.
[I, 483-493; p. 21]

Pope is on the side of *opifex rerum*, or "artist of the universe," and sees the Epicurean materialism and doctrine of chance as dullness and mindlessness. However, except in the *Essay on Man*, he seldom deals openly in cosmology but prefers to express himself in symbol and allegory and by allusion.

II

The best starting place for the exploration of the Creation theme in Pope is *Windsor Forest,* because it is an early poem, because the Ovidian influence on it is very strong, and because Wasserman's study in *The Subtler Language* has already displayed the all-pervading presence of *concordia discors.* He shows how the Forest is presented as a microcosm that forms "the symbolic scene in which and against which all the acts of the poem take place and from which they derive their special values" and that every episode — the account of the Normans, the hunts; the myth of Lodona; the description of the Thames; the retirement of Trumbull; the poet's flight to the Forest, his vision of earlier poets, and his meditation on old and recent history; Anne's achievement of the Peace of Utrecht; the epiphany and prophecy of the river god — springs from the cosmic harmony of the Forest expressed at the beginning of the poem. We can confirm Wasserman's analysis at many points by tracing the Ovidian pattern. Here first is the symbolic description of the Forest.

Here Hills and Vales, the Woodland and the Plain,
Here Earth and Water seem to strive again,
Not *Chaos*-like together crush'd and bruis'd,
But as the World, harmoniously confus'd:
Where Order in Variety we see,
And where, tho' all things differ, all agree.

Here waving Groves a checquer'd Scene display,
And part admit and part exclude the Day;
As some coy Nymph her Lover's warm Address
Nor quite indulges, nor can quite repress.
There, interspers'd in Lawns and opening Glades,
Thin Trees arise that shun each others Shades.
Here in full Light the russet Plains extend;
There wrapt in Clouds the blueish Hills ascend:
Ev'n the wild Heath displays her Purple Dies,
And 'midst the Desert fruitful Fields arise,
That crown'd with tufted Trees and springing Corn,
Like verdant Isles the sable Waste adorn.

[11-28]

This passage is often compared to the "strange varieties"
lines from Denham's *Cooper's Hill.*

Here Nature, whether more intent to please
Us or her self, with strange varieties,
(For things of wonder give no less delight
To the wise Maker's, than beholders sight.
Though these delights from several causes move
For so our children, thus our friends we love)
Wisely she knew, the harmony of things
As well as that of sounds, from discords springs.
Such was the discord, which did first disperse
Form, order, beauty through the Universe;
While driness moysture, coldness heat resists,
All that we have, and that we are, subsists.
While the steep horrid roughness of the Wood
Strives with the gentle calmness of the flood.
Such huge extreams when Nature doth unite,
Wonder from thence results, from thence delight.

[197-212]

Denham had begun the poem with an allusion to Ovid's lines on
Pythagoras in the *Metamorphoses* (XV, 60ff.), and in the quoted
passage he alludes to Ovid's Creation — witness his translation of
Ovid's line 19, "*frigida pugnabant calidis, umentia siccis.*" He
adapts Ovid's description of the globe, with its harmonious pattern of elements, to the woods and waters of the Forest landscape.

Pope follows him in this but restores the Creation passage to the beginning where it controls the whole poem. He recalls first the ordering of Chaos, then emphasizes at all points the harmonious contrast of the opposites of light and shade, high and low, barren and fertile, and so on, as Ovid had emphasized the interaction of land, water, air, and fire. There is some verbal resemblance between the couplet

> Here in full light the russet Plains extend;
> There wrapt in Clouds the blueish Hills ascend,

in which each word or phrase in the first line contrasts with the corresponding one in the second, yet the result is a harmonious whole, and

> Bids Trees increase to Woods, the Plaines extend,
> The rocky Mountaynes rise, and Vales descend,

a couplet Pope often echoes.

The most important lines of all are those that identify the features of the Forest landscape with the order of the elements and announce the theme of *concordia discors*:

> Here Hills and Vales, the Woodland and the Plain,
> Here Earth and Water seem to strive again,
> Not *Chaos*-like together crush'd and bruis'd,
> But as the World, harmoniously confus'd.
> Where Order in Variety we see,
> And where, tho' all things differ, all agree.

The last couplet takes its cosmological imagery from the account of the Empedoclean philosophy in the *Astronomica*,

> From whose agreeing disagreement springs
> The numerous odd Variety of Things,

and places the same emphasis on order. The fact that Creech is here translating Manilius's phrase *"discordia concors"* ("numer-

ous" here means "harmonious," and "odd" means "discrepant")
in itself is surely enough to prove the symbolic interpretation of
Pope's lines and hence even of the whole of *Windsor Forest*. So
Pope establishes the Forest-cosmos; and on the ancient analogy
the bodies and souls of the men who inhabit it will be composed of
the same Forest elements, and the full compass of their actions
and feelings will be expressible in Forest terms.

The next episode treads a delicate path through geography
and history to trace the coming of the Golden Age to England.
The inauspicious Norman creation of the New Forest is described
in reversed Ovidian language.

> Not thus the Land appear'd in Ages past,
> A dreary Desart and a gloomy Waste,
> To Savage Beasts and Savage Laws a Prey,
> And Kings more furious and severe than they:
> Who claim'd the Skies, dispeopled Air and Floods,
> The lonely Lords of empty Wilds and Woods.
>
> [43-48]

Compare this extract with Dryden's version of Ovid's account of
the creation of life,

> Then, every void of Nature to supply,
> With Forms of Gods he fills the vacant Skie:
> New Herds of Beasts he sends the Plains to share;
> New Colonies of Birds, to people Air;
> And to their Oozy Beds the finny Fish repair,
>
> [I, 72-75; i, 92-96]

and with one couplet from Sandys,

> The glittering Fishes to the Flouds repayre;
> The Beasts to Earth, the Birds resort to Ayre.
>
> [p. 2]

Notice, for example, "people" in Dryden and "dispeople" in
Pope, and "air" and "floods" in both Sandys and Pope. The

Normans counterwork God and create a "void of nature"; and not content with that, they "quit their sphere, and rush into the skies," seeking to dispossess God (the skies represent the ether, so that in one couplet Pope mentions all four elements). By refusing to remain within the limits fixed for them, the *limites certi* of Ovid's line 69, they work for the return of Chaos. In the manuscript, the fourth line of the extract read, "And Kings more boundless and more fierce than they"; the word "boundless," like the "due bounds" of *Essay on Man*, Epistle II, line 119, recalls Ovid's *limites*, and is, like line 52, "And ev'n the Elements a Tyrant sway'd," a sign of the cosmological mode.

In Ovid, God's act of Creation was immediately followed by the Golden Age, and the result of the uncreating acts of the Normans is to produce a reversal of the Golden Age. Here is Sandys:

> The *Golden Age* was first; which uncompeld,
> And without rule, in faith and Truth exceld.
> As then, there was nor punishment, nor feare;
> Nor threatning Lawes in brasse prescribed were;
> Nor suppliant crouching pris'ners shooke to see
> Their angrie Judge: but all was safe and free.
> . . . .
> Nor Swords, nor Armes, were yet: no Trenches round
> Besieged Townes, nor strifefull Trumpets sound:
> The Souldier, of no use. In firme content
> And harmlesse ease, their happy daies were spent.
> The yet-free Earth did of her owne accord
> (Untorne with ploughs) all sorts of fruit afford.
> . . . .
> 'Twas alwaies Spring: warme *Zephyrus* sweetly blew
> On smiling flowres, which without setting grew.
> Forth-with the Earth corne, unmanured, beares,
> And every yeere renewes her golden Eares.
>   [I, 89-93, 97-102, 107-110; p. 3]

"Then was there neither Master nor Servant," says Sandys's note, "names meerly brought in by ambition and injury. Unforced Nature gave sufficient to all; who securely possest her undivided bounty. A rich condition wherein no man was poore: Avarice after

introducing indigency: who by coveting a propriety, alienated all;
and lost what it had, by seeking to inlarge it" (p. 25).

Pope in ensuing lines inverts many of the details of this description; thus,

> What could be free, when lawless Beasts obey'd,
> And ev'n the Elements a Tyrant sway'd? [51-52]

> Our haughty *Norman* boasts that barb'rous Name,
> And makes his trembling Slaves the Royal Game. [63-64]

> Cities laid waste. . . . [49]

> The levell'd Towns with Weeds lie cover'd o'er,
> The hollow Winds thro' naked Temples roar. [67-68]

> In vain kind Seasons swell'd the teeming Grain. . . . [53]

> The Swain with Tears his frustrate Labour yields,
> And famish'd dies amidst his ripen'd Fields. [55-56]

But later the "golden years" came to England, and man was able
to live in the Forest harmoniously with Nature.

The next part of the poem describes field sports (lines 96-164),
and as Wasserman has observed, the ordered variety of the seasons
that form the pattern of this section is reinforced by the stress that
is placed upon the sportsmen's enjoyment of the elements. Indeed, the scheme is quite formal and Empedoclean, and it is worth
analyzing briefly as a guide to Pope's method in other passages.
The elements are introduced in turn to correspond to the seasons.
The autumnal partridge and pheasant shooting is associated with
earth. The spaniel lies couched close to the earth, and the par-
tridges, notoriously ground-loving birds (the myth of Perdix in
Book VIII of the *Metamorphoses* explains why "they never mount
aloft"), are netted while still feeding in the fields. The pheasant
succeeds in taking to the air but falls when shot, and as he dies,
"beats the Ground." The winter sport of coursing is followed

with "well-breath'd Beagles" — the adjective emphasizes air. The smaller birds shot in winter, doves, woodcock, lapwings, and larks, are shown in flight; and the section concludes by telling us how the last, the highest flying of all, "leave their little Lives in Air." In spring, there is fishing; and the last words of this season's section are "watry Plains," a periphrasis for water. The remaining element is introduced in the first line on the summer sport of stag hunting, "Now *Cancer* glows with *Phoebus'* fiery Car." This completes the pattern; and since fire may be the same as ether on occasion (for example, in Stanley's account of Empedocles), it also prepares the transition for the representation of Anne as an ethereal being, the moon, and for the appearance of the goddess Diana, who seeks the other three elements again (the grove, like the wood in the passage quoted from *Cooper's Hill*, represents the earth of which it is part).

> Here was she seen o'er Airy Wastes to rove,
> Seek the clear Spring, or haunt the pathless Grove.
>
> [167-168]

It was a triumph of Wasserman's criticism to redeem the story of Lodona, which follows in lines 171 to 218, from the disesteem into which Johnson's words "a ready and puerile expedient" had brought it. Wasserman showed that it is in fact the central point and epitome of the whole poem. The beauty whose praise and care Lodona scorns is in fact *concordia discors*. Straying outside the Forest limits, she quits the realm of concord and is attacked by Pan, who, as Wasserman shows from Bacon, stands for Chaos. Changed to a slow, winding stream, she is again contained by the Forest and she herself contains it, and the greater universe, in image; thus concord is restored in another form. This analysis, here most briefly summarized, can be supported by a look at the Creation references; for example, Lodona's eagerness for the chase is a sign that, to adapt a later Ovidian phrase of Pope's (compare "the selfe-poiz'd Earth"), the "balance of her mind" is not perfect but inclined toward the Empedoclean *neikos*, or "strife"; while "the Forest's verdant Limits" surely alludes to the *limites certi* (*Metamorphoses*, I, 69) with which Ovid's *opifex rerum* bounded the

parts of the Creation. In this passage, as elsewhere, we find several of the senses of *kosmos* recorded by Stephanus: such are the feminine adornment, or beauty, which Lodona scorns; the order (the basic meaning) which she disrupts by leaving the Forest limits; and the sky that she later reflects.

Creation references abound throughout the remainder of the poem. Trumbull "looks on Heav'n," recalling *dedit caelum videre (ibid.* 85); and his "Kindred Stars" recalls the *cognatum caelum (ibid.* 81) from which man's soul was made. Granville recreates Nature and makes the hills of Windsor rise, *lapidosos surgere montes (ibid.* 41), Sandys's "bids . . . the rocky Mountaynes rise." Other things that "rise" in the poem, sometimes, as in Sandys's prefatory verses, watched by the creator, are the peaceful cottage, the lofty woods, villas, temples, and Whitehall. The union of opposites is seen in the blending of earth and water in Windsor vaults and of the oppressor and the oppressed in the grave; in the qualities of the tributaries, swift, slow, dark, chalky, transparent, sedgy, which flow into the Thames; and in the villas' dark shadows that fall on the crystal stream. The Thames, the great unifying symbol of the poem, is, like the rivers of the Creation, a river with winding banks. That the seas really join what they seem to divide is perhaps a sign of the dominance of the unitive Empedoclean love over the discretive strife.

Nothing has been said yet of the political meaning of the poem, so well expounded by Wasserman, who traces the analogies between the harmony of the Forest and the peace achieved by Anne. Yet the Creation also can easily take on a political meaning. It is hard to believe that the readers of the *Metamorphoses* were not intended to see a parallel between the divine pacification of the elements at the beginning of the poem, when

> God, or Nature, while they thus contend,
> To these intestine Discords put an end,
> [I, 21; Dryden's translation, 25-26]

and the pacification to be achieved by Augustus, which is prophesied at the end of the last book,

> Peace given to Earth; he shall convert his care
> To civill Rule, just Lawes.
>
> > [XV, 832-833; Sandys's translation, p. 509]

As W. Y. Sellar puts it, "The same power which had worked so many miracles in the morning of the world, is again, in these later times, made visible in connection with the central fact and dominant sentiment of the age, the elevation of Augustus to supreme power and divine honours" (*The Roman Poets of the Augustan Age: Horace and the Elegiac Poets*). Stephanus also juxtaposes the cosmological and the political in his definition of *akosmia*, the opposite of *kosmos*:

> A disturbed state of things . . . Plutarch called the state of the Roman republic at the time of the civil war *akosmia*, which he opposed to *eukosmia* [good order]. Again, Budaeus translates *akosmia* in Aristotle's *De Mundo* as a confused and disorderly mass . . . for so he interprets these words . . . "And it is more suitable to call the universe itself a *kosmos*, that is a structure which is settled and arranged in fitting order, than an *akosmia*, that is a confused and disorderly mass."[1]

Stephanus then cites a use of the word in the sense of "Chaos." Pope may also have remembered Shakespeare's use of Ovidian phrases in a political context in *King John*:

> > you are born
> > To set a form upon that indigest
> > Which he hath left so shapeless and so rude.
> >
> > > [V, vii, 25-27]

Many years later in his *Epistle to Bathurst* Pope would use disorder in the four elements as a symbol of disorder in the state.

> At length Corruption, like a gen'ral flood,
> (So long by watchful Ministers withstood)
> Shall deluge all; and Av'rice creeping on,
> Spread like a low-born mist, and blot the Sun.
>
> > [137-140]

The England of Walpole and George II was to be taken as out of

harmony with God's design, as the England of Oxford and Anne was in it. Pope likens Anne's achievements to Augustus's not only by imitating the *Georgics* and by the ambiguous "Augusta" of line 377, "Behold! *Augusta*'s glitt'ring Spires increase," which could mean either London or Anne, but again in the very lines that describe the crowning act of her beneficent reign:

> What Tears has *Albion* shed,
> Heav'ns! what new Wounds, and how her old have bled?
> She saw her Sons with purple Deaths expire,
> Her sacred Domes involv'd in rolling Fire,
> A dreadful Series of Intestine Wars,
> Inglorious Triumphs, and dishonest Scars.
> At length great *ANNA* said — Let Discord cease!
> She said, the World obey'd, and all was *Peace*!
>
> [321-328]

The concluding couplet echoes the fiat of Genesis and also, by its reference to discord, seems to invoke the classical doctrine of Creation; at the same time it alludes to the praise of Augustus at the end of Book I of the *Astronomica* (the subject is comets):

> They Civil-Wars foretell, and Brothers rage,
> *The Curse and the Disgraces of an Age.*
> Never more *Comets* drew their dreadfull Hair
> Than when *Philippi* saw the World at War.
> Scarce had the Plains drunk up the former Bloud,
> On scatter'd Bones and Limbs the *Romans* stood
> And fought again; disdaining meaner Foes,
> (A wretched Conquest where the Victors lose)
> Our *Empire*'s power did its own self oppose.
> . . . .
> Let this, O Fates! suffice; Let *Discord* cease,
> And raging Tumults be confin'd by Peace.
> Let *Caesar* triumph, let the World obey,
> And long let *Rome* be happy in his sway.
> Long have him here, and when she shall bestow
> A *God* on Heaven enjoy his Aid below.
>
> [I, 906-912, 921-926; p. 36]

Some evidence of another kind for this cosmological inter-

pretation of *Windsor Forest* is perhaps to be found in complimentary verses written by Francis Knapp and dated June 1715. Knapp, an Oxonian of Magdalen, where he was contemporary with Addison, dwells on the cosmological aspects of the poem and recognizes Pope as the creator of *concordia discors*, an *opifex rerum*.

> Nor half so true the fair Lodona shows
> The sylvan state that on her border grows.
> . . . .
> Thy juster lays the lucid wave surpass;
> The living scene is in the Muse's glass.
> Nor sweeter notes the ecchoing Forests chear,
> When Philomela sits and warbles there,
> Than when you sing the greens, and opening glades,
> And give us *Harmony* as well as Shades.
> . . . .
>   With *vast variety* thy pages shine;
> A *new creation* starts in ev'ry line.
> How sudden trees rise to the reader's sight,
> And make a doubtful scene of shade and light,
> And give at once the day, at once the night!
> And here again what *sweet confusion* reigns,
> In dreary deserts mix'd with painted plains!
>
>   [My italics]

Addressing the Atlantic, he reverses Denham's famous lines on the Thames.

> Let me ne'er flow like thee! nor make thy stream
> My sad example, or my wretched theme.
> Like bombast now thy raging billows roar,
> And vainly dash themselves against the shore:
> About like quibbles now thy froth is thrown,
> And *all extreams* are in a moment shown.

In addressing the Thames itself, he picks up Pope's description of the tributaries.

> From *various* springs divided waters glide,
> In diff'rent colours roll a diff'rent tyde,

> Murmur along their *crooked banks* a while,
> At once they murmur and enrich the Isle;
> A while distinct thro' many channels run,
> But meet at last, and *sweetly* flow in *one*.

The interpretation suggested by these lines seems to have met with Pope's approval, since he printed them in the 1717 edition of his *Works*.

III

It is easy and natural to compare human and divine creation and to show the artist as being like God, or God as an artist. This way of thought was established hundreds, if not thousands, of years before Ovid, who implies it when he uses expressions like *opifex rerum* and *mundi fabricator*; and once he had provided such a detailed description of the Creation, later poets of literary bent often drew their metaphors from him. A good example is in Dryden's *Song for St. Cecilia's Day*, where the "heap of jarring atoms" is Ovid's *rudis indigestaque moles* and where we find also the opposites of "hot and cold and moist and dry." Again in a poem about music, the ode on Purcell's death, Dryden tells how the "godlike man" would have "tuned the jarring sphere" of Hell — the cosmological language will be recognized. The first book of the *Davideis* contains a remarkably faithful imitation of Ovid, which proves, among other things, that Cowley did not know when he had said enough, and which amused Johnson:

> As first a various unform'd *Hint* we find
> Rise in some god-like *Poets* fertile *Mind*,
> Till all the parts and words their places take,
> And with just marches *verse* and *musick* make;
> Such was *Gods Poem*, this *Worlds* new *Essay*;
> So wild and rude in its first draught it lay;
> Th' ungovern'd parts no *Correspondence* knew,
> An artless *war* from thwarting *Motions* grew;
> Till they to *Number* and fixt Rules were brought

By the eternal *Minds Poetique Thought.*
Water and *Air* he for the *Tenor* chose,
Earth made the *Base*, the *Treble Flame* arose.

[447-458]

The parts and words that take their places correspond to the elements, and the "just marches" are no doubt the *limites certi* of
Ovid's line 69. In the second part of the comparison, "wild and
rude" translates *rudis indigestaque*, "no *Correspondence* knew"
refers to *non bene iunctarum*, and the "artless *war*" is the strife of
the opposites.

Of course other cosmological sources could be used in the
same way. Dryden, in his *Epistle to Sir Robert Howard*, trans-
mutes the old argument between Stoic and Epicurean, applying it
to Howard's poetry:

this is a piece too fair
To be the child of Chance, and not of Care,
No Atoms casually together hurl'd
Could e're produce so beautifull a world.
Nor dare I such a doctrine here admit,
As would destroy the providence of wit.

[29-34]

This is in fact a borrowing from the previously quoted passage of
the *Astronomica* in which Manilius uses the argument from design to attack Epicureanism.

It must be *God*, nor was it made by *Chance*;
As *Epicurus* dreamt. He madly thought
This beauteous Frame of heedless *Atoms* wrought.

Pope has several such passages describing artistic endeavor;
but first we should examine his treatment of aesthetic theory,
chiefly in the *Essay on Criticism*. The *Essay* may seem a perspicu-
ous work, whose main claim to originality lies in the superlative
expression of time-honored critical doctrines. However, I believe
that it has another claim, and that Pope imbued his material with

cosmological allusions so as to endow it with a second range of meaning apart from that which appears on the surface. This may perhaps be the explanation of his view that it was a difficult work, witness his remark, quoted by Johnson with eloquent lack of comment, that "not one gentleman in sixty, even of liberal education," could understand it. We may begin by looking at the word *criticism* itself. The sense in which Pope used it was then fairly recent and had been defined by Dryden as "judging well." Stephanus defines the root word *krino* as "Separate, decide, set asunder. For I think that this is the first sense, and not judge. The latter is more likely to have arisen from the former, since obviously *krinein* was säid for *krinein neikea* (an expression also found in Homer), that is, to decide disputes. For to judge is to decide disputes."[2] The phrase *dirimere lites*, which has here been translated as "decide disputes," has only one classical occurrence — when Ovid describes how God and Nature ended the strife of Chaos, *"hanc deus et melior litem natura diremit"* (*Metamorphoses* I, 21); and the Greek *neikos*, which Stephanus translates as *lis*, is also Empedocles's strife. This definition therefore strongly suggests that criticism is a cosmological or ordering activity.

To Pope, criticism is one of the arts and therefore requires skill in its exercise. He even quotes Pliny to the effect that only a painter can judge painting, a sculptor sculpture, and so on; and although he does not seem to maintain this position very rigorously, nevertheless much of the *Essay* is directed to critics and artists alike. The first commandment is,

> First follow NATURE, and your Judgment frame
> By her just Standard, which is still the same.
> *Unerring Nature*, still divinely bright,
> One *clear, unchang'd*, and *Universal* Light.
>
> [68-71]

One may sympathize with Dennis who complained that Pope did not make it clear what it was to judge or to write in accordance with Nature. But as the Twickenham note points out, Nature here is all but explicitly identified with God; and Sandys was quite

explicit in his translation of the *Metamorphoses* and his first note (although he is not justified by the text on this point). Ovid, he says,

> confesseth God, not disguizing his name . . . to be the Creator of the World. . . . Whom he also calleth the *Better Nature*; so named by the Stoicke: *Wilt thou call him Nature? Thou offendest not: it is he by whose spirit wee live, of whom all things were borne.* The better concludes a worse, which was *Chaos*: God they held to be the Minde, and *Chaos* the Matter.

What God and Nature did was to separate, arrange, harmonize, and bound the matter of the universe, and writers and critics must also separate, arrange, harmonize, and bound, and look to an ordered whole. Or if Nature is taken, as Pope sometimes seems to take it, to mean the created universe rather than the Creator, it makes no practical difference to his meaning since Nature then provides the model of the work of art finished on these principles.

The *Essay*, especially near the beginning, describes the critical scene as having certain resemblances to Chaos. Some are bewildered and lost in the maze; some lose their common sense, a form of *nous*; some change from fool to coxcomb, or from wit to poet to critic to fool, just as in Chaos there was "no certaine forme to any one assign'd" (*nulli sua forma manebat*). But the jarring seeds of judgment, disordered by false learning, pride, a love to parts and so on, may be ordered again by an intellectual act. The would-be critic is to distinguish sense from dullness, know his own limits, end the strife between wit and judgment (which should be like man and wife, marriage being a symbol of the harmony of the elements), and bound his faculties. This is a cosmological process.

A particularly important passage is that on "young Maro," where Pope claims that the revered rules that Aristotle "discovered not devised" are ordained by Nature.

> When first young *Maro* in his boundless Mind
> A Work t'outlast Immortal *Rome* design'd,

> Perhaps he seem'd *above* the Critick's Law,
> And but from *Nature's Fountains* scorn'd to draw:
> But when t'examine ev'ry Part he came,
> *Nature* and *Homer* were, he found, the *same*:
> Convinc'd, amaz'd, he checks the bold Design,
> And Rules as strict his labour'd Work confine,
> As if the *Stagyrite* o'erlook'd each Line.
> Learn hence for Ancient *Rules* a just Esteem;
> To copy *Nature* is to copy *Them*.
>
> [130-140]

Virgil is here shown engaged in creation, attempting a work that would last for eternity. His own mind is boundless, but when he examines (that is, ponders or weighs) his work in detail, he sees the need to check and confine it with strict rules. This process resembles the manner in which God ordered the universe and bounded it with *limites certi*, and it is noticeable that "But when t'examine ev'ry Part he came" is exceedingly close to Sandys's "And every part to due proportion brought" both in form and sense. The claim that Homer and Aristotle's rules are the same as Nature is openly cosmological.

Even more important, because they contain the very core of Pope's aesthetic doctrine, are the following lines:

> In Wit, as Nature, what affects our Hearts
> Is not th' Exactness of peculiar Parts;
> 'Tis not a *Lip*, or *Eye*, we Beauty call,
> But the joint Force and full *Result* of *All*.
> Thus when we view some well-proportion'd Dome,
> (The *World*'s just Wonder, and ev'n *thine* O *Rome*!)
> No single Parts unequally surprize;
> All comes *united* to th' admiring Eyes;
> No monstrous Height, or Breadth, or Length appear;
> The *Whole* at once is *Bold*, and *Regular*.
>
> [243-252]

The first two couplets reflect a note of Sandys's:

Now beauty consists not only (as some imagine) in the favour of

the face and delicacy of the complection; but in the dignitie of
the stature, the apt composition of the limbs, and harmonious
summetry of the lineaments: whose smallest discord is forthwith
apprehended by the eye, and as soone distasted. The face is to be
thrice the length of the nose. . . . Eight times the length of the
face should be the length of the body, of equall breadth when the
armes are displayed, [p. 366]

and so on. Sandys's note in turn is highly Vitruvian. His threefold
division of beauty recalls Vitruvius's definition of architecture as
order or *taxis*, arrangement or *diathesis*, and proportion and
symmetry or *oeconomia*.[3] His bodily measurements in the main
correspond to those that Vitruvius gives as the proper basis for the
proportions of temples.[4] Renaissance architectural theorists had
connected the Vitruvian proportions with the discoveries attributed to Pythagoras about the tensions and lengths of strings
which would produce musical intervals. These ratios were held to
lie at the basis of all beauty and *concordia discors*, and ultimately
of all existence. The theories had been carried to their conclusion
by Palladio, the guiding architectural spirit of Pope's age, who
had sought to relate all the parts of his buildings to one another
and to the whole in musical ratios.[5] Pope's architectural simile
shows his interest in the idea of beauty as proportion. He has
given the passage a further cosmological meaning by modeling
the last three couplets on Ovid's description of the fashioning of
the earth, which we may see translated by Sandys and Dryden respectively (the italics in each extract are mine):

> What God soever this division wrought,
> And every part to *due proportion* brought;
> First, least the Earth *unequall* should appeare,
> He turn'd it round, in figure of a Spheare.

and

> Thus when the God, what ever God was he,
> Had form'd the *whole*, and made the *parts agree*,
> That no *unequal portions* might be found,
> He moulded Earth into a spacious round.

[40-43]

Pope's favorite cosmological word *united* also appears and recalls the "unitive" force of creative love, or *philotēs*. Other cosmological references in the theoretical parts of the *Essay* include "From *vulgar Bounds* with *brave Disorder* part"; that is, only a master hand can rightly draw the *limites certi*, which when drawn by the vulgar may be transgressed with *discordia concors*; and possibly also the line on Homer "Still with *It self compar'd*, his *Text* peruse," which may allude to a line of Manilius on the "godlike" spherical form of the globe, "Alike and equal to its self 'tis found" (I, 213, p. 11). There is no need to collect every one of these references, but one last one is of interest. The lines on the ancient poets,

> Still green with Bays each *ancient* Altar stands,
> Above the reach of *Sacrilegious* Hands,
> Secure from *Flames*, from *Envy's* fiercer Rage,
> Destructive *War*, and all-devouring *Age*,[6]
>
> [181-184]

imitate a passage of Manilius describing the unchanging universe:

> Yet safe the World, and free from Change doth last,
> No Years encrease it, and no Years can waste;
> Its course it urges on, and keeps its Frame,
> And still will be, because 'twas still the same.
> It stands secure from *Time*'s devouring Rage,
> For 'tis a *God*, nor can it change with Age.
>
> [I, 518-523; p. 22]

Pope several times imitates these lines, as in the *Essay* itself when he refers to Nature's "just standard which is still the same."

Such passages as these show the artist as, like the Creator, *kosmētikos*, defined by Stephanus as *"Ornandi peritus. Vel potius, ordinandi peritus, ab altera verbi [kosmein] significatione"*; that is, "skilled in adorning, or rather, skilled in ordering, from the other meaning of *kosmein*." The definition of *kosmein* is *"Inconditam rerum seriem in ordinem redigere: unde et pro Mun-*

dum architectari," or "To put a confused mass of things in order;
and so also to design the universe." But of course there are many
bad artists who lack the faculty of ordering their material aright
and whose creations will keep something of the marks of Chaos
about them. The principle prevailing in such unsatisfactory creations we may call *akosmia* or perhaps *kosmos akosmos*, both of
which occur under Stephanus's main article on *kosmos*. *Kosmos
akosmos* could have various meanings, according to the meanings of *kosmos* itself: disorderly order, disorderly world, world
that is no world, ugly beauty, and so on. It is found in a Sibylline
verse quoted by Stephanus, *"estai kosmos akosmos, apollumenōn
anthrōpōn"* or "the world shall be no world when mankind per-
ishes." *Akosmos* itself is defined as *inordinatus, indigestus,* or *in-
compositus,* among other things; the second, of course, immediately recalls *rudis indigestaque moles.* There can be little doubt
that a translator of Greek would sooner or later have occasion to
look up this article; Pope, for example, would have encountered
akosmos in the description of Thersites in Book II of the Iliad and
would probably have wished to assure himself of the exact force of
the word. At all events, the influence of these definitions seems to
appear strongly in such a passage as the following:

> Some to *Conceit* alone their Taste confine,
> And glitt'ring Thoughts struck out at ev'ry Line;
> Pleas'd with a Work where nothing's just or fit;
> One *glaring Chaos* and *wild Heap* of *Wit*:
> Poets like Painters, thus, unskill'd to trace
> The *naked Nature* and the *living Grace,*
> With *Gold* and *Jewels* cover ev'ry Part,
> And hide with *Ornaments* their *Want of Art.*
> *True Wit* is *Nature* to Advantage drest.

> [289-297]

The "wild Heap" is the *rudis indigestaque moles* that the poet of
conceit has been unable, through lack of the power of ordering, to
transmute into cosmos. Such poets, like the unskilled painters
("unskilled" here seems to reverse Stephanus's *ordinandi peritus*)
are "cosmetic" in Stephanus's first sense of ornamentation, but
only the possessors of true wit are cosmetic in the second, better

sense of skill in ordering, or dressing, Nature. *Akosmia* is a more subtle concept than the mere destructiveness of the Normans in *Windsor Forest*, which is depicted by the simple reversal of Creation language, and it appealed to Pope more strongly as he became more of a satirist.

A later passage in the *Essay* again opposes true creativity to *akosmia*.

> But most by *Numbers* judge a Poet's Song,
> And *smooth* or *rough*, with them, is *right* or *wrong*;
> In the bright *Muse* tho' thousand *Charms* conspire,
> Her *Voice* is all these tuneful Fools admire.
> . . . .
> These *Equal Syllables* alone require,
> Tho' oft the Ear the *open Vowels* tire,
> While *Expletives* their feeble Aid *do* join,
> And ten low Words oft creep in one dull Line,
> While they ring round the same *unvary'd Chimes*,
> With sure *Returns* of still *expected Rhymes*.
> . . . .
> Leave such to tune their own dull Rhimes, and know
> What's *roundly smooth*, or *languishingly slow*;
> And praise the *Easie Vigor* of a Line,
> Where *Denham*'s Strength, and *Waller*'s Sweetness join.
> True Ease in writing comes from Art, not Chance,
> As those move easiest who have learn'd to dance.
> . . . .
> Hear how *Timotheus*' various [later "vary'd"] Lays surprize,
> And bids Alternate Passions fall and rise!
> While, at each Change, the Son of *Lybian Jove*
> Now *burns* with Glory, and then *melts* with Love;
> Now his *fierce Eyes* with *sparkling Fury* glow;
> Now *Sighs* steal out, and *Tears begin to flow*.
> . . . .
> *The Pow'r of Musick* all our Hearts allow;
> And what *Timotheus* was, is *Dryden* now.
>   Avoid Extreams.
>   [337-340, 344-349, 358-363, 374-379, 382-384]

The key phrase in this passage is that which contrasts art and

chance, the former representing the Stoic view of Creation, the latter the Epicurean. The inept poets whom the inept critics admire have not the mental capacity of uniting different ingredients, the "thousand charms" of art. To echo Creech's phrase, their works are not numerous, since they tire the ear; nor odd, through lack of opposition between syllables and between words; nor do they have variety, since the same rhymes are repeated. A trace of Chaos remains in the ill-joined expletives and monosyllables (not that Pope "condemns monosyllabic lines," as has been carelessly said). They can obtain any good effects only by chance, like the "haughty dunces" in Dryden's *Prologue to the University of Oxford* (1673), who

> build their Poems the *Lucretian* way;
> So many Huddled Atoms make a Play,
> And if they hit in Order by some Chance,
> They call that Nature which is Ignorance.
>
> [32-35]

The true poets have the art and knowledge to blend different qualities such as smoothness, slowness, and vigor, and "join" the opposites of strength and sweetness. Timotheus commands a "numerous odd variety" and controls the passions as God controlled the elements, "bidding" them rise and fall. Fire, air, and water are mentioned in the description of Alexander's emotions, reminding us that "passions are the elements of life."

Further examples of artistic *akosmia* may be found in the *Epistle to Burlington*, which is closely related to the *Essay*, as many verbal resemblances, including the opening, show. Thus the Epicurean approach is shown by the "imitating fools" who, by taking "random drawings," that is, by relying on chance, shatter Burlington's "one beauty" into many blunders and arrange everything wrong,

> Load some vain Church with old Theatric state,
> Turn Arcs of triumph to a Garden-gate;

Reverse your Ornaments, and hang them all
On some patch'd dog-hole ek'd with ends of wall,

[29-32]

and so on. Burlington's "one beauty" and his "Ornaments" are, or could be, both translations of *kosmos,* and since *kosmos* also translates "world," it is possible that "reverse your Ornaments" is also intended to depict the destructive urge of those who would "invert the world" (see *Essay on Man,* III, 244).

From the theoretical passages we may pass to some which are more descriptive. In Pope's view, the supreme literary example of cosmic creation was probably the forging of the shield of Achilles in Book XVIII of the Iliad. The shield depicts heaven, ocean, and earth, with scenes of peace and war, rural occupations, singing, dancing, and so on. A curiosity of the description is that it can be read as being of a miraculous shield, in which the figures actually move, an interpretation that Pope firmly rejected. In the course of time, the shield became quite a philosophical object. Pope's note to line 537 of his translation quotes a theory whose immediate source was Eustathius but whose antecedents, it was said, go back to Pythagoras's daughter, that the four metals of the shield — gold, silver, tin, and brass — represented the elements. Pope goes on to point out that Homer names land, sky, and sea expressly,

> to which, for the fourth Element, you must add *Vulcan,* who makes the Shield. . . . To bring the matter of the Shield to Separation and Form, Vulcan presides over the Work, or as we may say, an *essential Warmth: All things,* says *Heraclitus, being made by the operation of Fire.* . . . And because the *Architect* is at this time to give a Form and Ornament to the World he is making, it is not rashly that he is said to be married to one of the Graces.

He suggests that the scenes of war and peace in the shield are the source of Empedocles's "assertion that all Things had their Original from *Strife* and *Friendship.*"

Pope's translation carries the cosmologizing of the shield a

little further. Two touches in particular may be mentioned. In writing "There shone the Image of the Master Mind" (line 557), he seems to allude to Genesis and also to a phrase of Creech's that became a favorite of his in Creation passages.

> In *Man* the God descends, and joys to find
> The narrow Image of his greater Mind.
>
> [II, 108; p. 53]

Again, at the end of the description of the shield, Pope writes,

> Thus the broad Shield complete the Artist crown'd
> With his last Hand, and pour'd the Ocean round:
> In living Silver seem'd the Waves to roll,
> And beat the Buckler's Verge, and bound the whole.
>
> [xviii, 701-704]

The beating of the waves, which is not in Homer, suggests Sandys's note to line 14 of Ovid, "*Amphitrite . . .* the name derived from the beating upon the incompassed Earth with her surges." Vulcan, then, follows the Maker of the universe in his own act of creation; but the real creator of the shield is, of course, Homer, from whose mind it all sprang. The whole process of selection, separation, ordering, and bounding is his, and in this way it can be said that Homer and creative Nature are the same.

In the same way, the painter forms a "bright Creation" on his canvas.

> So when the faithful *Pencil* has design'd
> Some *bright Idea* of the Master's Mind,
> Where a *new World* leaps out at his command,
> And ready Nature waits upon his Hand;
> When the ripe Colours *soften* and *unite*,
> And sweetly *melt* into just Shade and Light,
> When mellowing Years their full Perfection give,
> And each Bold Figure just begins to *Live*.
>
> [*Essay on Criticism*, 484-491]

Here too we see the idea, or image, of the artist's mind, Nature as the partner of the creator (*deus et melior natura*), the harmonizing of the opposites into shade and light, and the appearance of life. Jervas acts similarly.

> Whether thy hand strike out some free design,
> Where life awakes, and dawns at ev'ry line;
> Or blend in beauteous tints the colour'd mass. . . .
> [*Epistle to Mr. Jervas*, 3-5]

The "coloured mass" of pigments from which Jervas creates the picture probably reflects Sandy's "that blinde Masse" (translating *caeco acervo* in Ovid's line 24), and hence corresponds to matter as it was in Chaos.

The gardener also must follow the *opifex rerum*, as we see in the *Epistle to Burlington*.

> Consult the Genius of the Place in all;
> That tells the Waters or to rise, or fall,
> Or helps th' ambitious Hill the heav'n to scale,
> Or scoops in circling theatres the Vale,
> . . . .
> Joins willing woods.
> [57-60, 62]

Or again,

> Behold Villario's ten-years toil compleat;
> His Quincunx darkens, his Espaliers meet,
> The Wood supports the Plain, the parts unite,
> And strength of Shade contends with strength of Light;
> A waving Glow his bloomy beds display,
> Blushing in bright diversities of day,
> With silver-quiv'ring rills mæander'd o'er.
> [79-85]

These two extracts may be compared with Sandys's lines from the opening of the *Metamorphoses*,

To those he addeth Springs, Ponds, Lakes immense;
And Rivers, whom their winding borders fence.
. . . .
Bids Trees increase to Woods, the Plaines extend,
The rocky Mountaynes rise, and Vales descend.

To Burlington is indeed highly cosmological throughout. It contains a triumphantly successful use of the Ovidian Creation form to portray *kosmos akosmos*.

At Timon's villa let us pass a day,
Where all cry out, "What sums are thrown away!"
So proud, so grand, of that stupendous air,
Soft and Agreeable come never there.
Greatness, with Timon, dwells in such a draught
As brings all Brobdignag before your thought.
To compass this, his building is a Town,
His pond an Ocean, his parterre a Down:
Who but must laugh, the Master when he sees,
A puny insect, shiv'ring at a breeze!
Lo, what huge heaps of littleness around!
The whole, a labour'd Quarry above ground.
Two Cupids squirt before: a Lake behind
Improves the keenness of the Northern wind.
His Gardens next your admiration call,
On ev'ry side you look, behold the Wall!
No pleasing Intricacies intervene,
No artful wildness to perplex the scene;
Grove nods at grove, each Alley has a brother,
And half the platform just reflects the other.
The suff'ring eye inverted Nature sees,
Trees cut to Statues, Statues thick as trees,
With here a Fountain, never to be play'd,
And there a Summer-house, that knows no shade;
Here Amphitrite sails thro' myrtle bow'rs;
There Gladiators fight, or die, in flow'rs;
Un-water'd see the drooping sea-horse mourn,
And swallows roost in Nilus' dusty Urn.

[99-126]

Pope starts by telling us that Timon has no artistic power. Horace had written, in famous words,

molle atque facetum
Vergilio adnuerunt gaudentes rure Camenae,
[*Satires*, I, x, 44-45]

"the Muses who love the countryside have granted the soft and the agreeable to Virgil." The same Muses have not so favored Timon, and he cannot therefore succeed in his attempt to create landscape by architecture and gardening. The description of the villa and the gardens is merciless; and upon analysis we can see that this passage is an elaborate allusion to the opening of the *Metamorphoses*, with Timon the *opifex rerum* who creates a *kosmos akosmos*, one mark of which is his faulty arrangement of the elements. Let us take water first. Timon's property is in two parts, the villa and the gardens; the villa, which does not need water, has the lake and the Cupids, and the gardens, which do, have none. The lake is in the wrong place, behind the house, and does not temper the cold wind but makes it colder; the Cupids are doing with water in front of the house what should not be done with it there. Pope mentions the lack of water in the gardens at just those three points where it is not merely required for the natural growth of plants but is essential to the garden design: a fountain should play; a sea horse should be set in water, not remind us by wilting that it is on dry land; and an urn representing a river should run. Earth is out of place or misused in the house itself (a quarry above ground), in the undue abundance of stone statues, perhaps in the topiary (trees and woods are a symbol of earth in *Cooper's Hill*), and in the dust in the urn, where water should be. The last line is more pointed than may appear. The swallows come from Egypt to nest in England and find the Nile here — but a dry Nile. This absurdity recalls the *Dunciad* "Realms shift their place, and Ocean turns to land" (I, 72). Air, in the form of the North Wind, is out of harmony with water, which makes its coldness even colder; and Timon, who shivers at a summer breeze, is out of harmony with air. Fire is represented by the sun on the summerhouse, where it should be blended with shade but is not.

The opposites, too, are mishandled. The house and pond are too big; the parterre is too big and is high, "a Down," when it should be low; littleness is made huge. Timon is too little, an

insect, not a man. In the gardens the harmony of opposites is lacking because there is no opposition: "grove nods at grove," and so
forth. There is no "artful wildness," words that translate *discordia concors.*

The couplet about Amphitrite and the gladiators is especially rich in cosmological meaning. We must first understand
that, by one of Pope's most sardonic strokes, Timon has placed
Amphitrite among myrtles because — misled by the similarity of
name — he has mistaken her for Aphrodite, who of course has the
myrtle as her sacred tree. So now the sea-goddess is absurdly standing in a wood; we may perhaps be meant to remember that Ovid
uses her name in his description of Chaos, where she was also out
of place. Worse, while failing to put love in her proper place, he
has found two places for strife, represented by the fighting and
dying gladiators. The whole scene is a failure of art and a reversal
of Sandys's verses,

> FIRE, AIRE, EARTH, WATER, all the Opposites
> That strove in *Chaos,* powrefull LOVE unites,
> And from their Discord drew this Harmonie,
> Which smiles in *Nature:* who, with ravisht eye,
> Affects his owne-made *Beauties,*

and so the eye that sees inverted Nature is a suffering, not a ravished, one.[7]

The *akosmia* which reigns in Timon's little world is evident
in his decorations (he is neither *ornandi peritus* nor *ordinandi
peritus*), his furnishings, his books, his worship, his dinner, everything: yet Pope is careful to tell us that this discordant microcosm
is part of the greater harmony, and will return to it:

> Yet hence the Poor are cloath'd, the Hungry fed;
> Health to himself, and to his Infants bread
> The Lab'rer bears: What his hard Heart denies,
> His charitable Vanity supplies.
>   Another age shall see the golden Ear
> Imbrown the Slope, and nod on the Parterre,

Deep Harvests bury all his pride has plann'd,
And laughing Ceres re-assume the land.

[169-172]

The end of the poem is a tribute to the creative powers
of landowners like Bathurst and of Burlington, built around
Sandys's couplet

Bids Trees increase to Woods, bids Plaines extend,
The rocky Mountaynes rise, and Vales descend.

The landowner is to plant,

Let his plantations stretch from down to down,
First shade a Country, and then raise a Town.

[189-190]

Burlington is to provide artificial structures corresponding to the
natural structures with which God adorned the globe,

You too proceed! make falling Arts your care,
Erect new wonders, and the old repair,
Jones and Palladio to themselves restore,
And be whate'er Vitruvius was before:
Till Kings call forth th' Idea's of your mind,
Proud to accomplish what such hands design'd,
Bid Harbors open, public Ways extend,
Bid Temples, worthier of the God, ascend;
Bid the broad Arch the dang'rous Flood contain,
The Mole projected break the roaring Main;
Back to his bounds their subject Sea command,
And roll obedient Rivers thro' the Land;
These Honours, Peace to happy Britain brings,
These are Imperial Works, and worthy Kings.

[191-204]

He is also to separate and harmonize the elements of earth and
water much as God did. It seems possible that he is compared with
creative Nature in the line "Erect new wonders, and the old repair," since it echoes Manilius's attack on Epicurus, who

madly thought
This beauteous Frame of heedless *Atoms* wrought,
That Seas and Earth, the Stars and spacious Air,
Which forms New Worlds, or doth the Old repair,
First rose from these.

The effects that Epicurus attributes to chance Pope attributes to Burlington's mind. We may also compare the lines on Burlington's ordering of land and water ("Bid the broad Arch," and so on) with Sandys's

Then, Seas diffus'd; commanding them to roar
With ruffling Winds, and give the Land a shore.
To those he addeth Spring, Ponds, Lakes immense;
And Rivers, whom their winding borders fence.

Pope uses "bid" three times and "command" once in a very few lines, a reflection of Ovid's repeated *iussit,* about which Sandys writes, as we saw earlier,

He confesseth God to be the Creator of the World and maker of all things: and by that word *Commanded,* so often reiterated, that hee made them by his Word only . . . God they held to be the Minde, and *Chaos* the matter: the Minde called by *Pluto* the worlds Architectresse.

In Pope's own reiteration of the same word we again seem to find a recondite but magnificent compliment to the Palladian Earl and his godlike art.

IV

Timon's failure was not only aesthetic; fundamentally it was moral and appeared in his self-centeredness and pride. The *akosmia* of his architecture and gardening merely reflects that of his soul. The use of Ovidian language to express moral order or disorder was not new in English poetry. Clifford echoed Ovid when he abused Richard Plantagenet in *Henry VI, Part 2,*

Hence, heap of wrath, foul indigested lump,
As crooked in thy manners as thy shape;
[V, i, 157-158]

and the Bastard in *King John* rails at

Commodity, the bias of the world;
The world, who of itself is peised well,
[II, i, 574-575]

recalling *tellus ponderibus librata suis*. A more schematic application is found in Spenser's *Hymne in Honour of Love*.

The earth, the ayre, the water, and the fyre,
Then gan to raunge them selves in huge array,
And with contrary forces to conspyre
Each against other, by all meanes they may,
Threatning their owne confusion and decay:
Ayre hated earth, and water hated fyre,
Till Love relented their rebellious yre.

He then them tooke, and tempering goodly well
Their contrary dislikes with loved meanes,
Did place them all in order, and compell
To keepe them selves within their sundrie raines,
Together linkt with Adamantine chaines;
Yet so, as that in every living wight
They mixe themselves, and shew their kindly might.
[78-91]

Sandys, it will be remembered, had written,

FIRE, AIRE, EARTH, WATER, all the Opposites
That strove in *Chaos*, powrefull LOVE unites.
. . . .
        But, our *Will*,
Desire, and *Powres Irascible*, the skill
Of PALLAS orders; who the *Mind* attires
With all *Heroick Vertues*,

comparing the ordering of the passions by Pallas with the order-

ing of the elements. Pope, of course, explicitly states that the passions are the elements of life, which must be ordered by the God within the mind.

> Passions, like Elements, tho' born to fight,
> Yet, mix'd and soften'd, in his work unite:
> These 'tis enough to temper and employ;
> But what composes Man, can Man destroy?
> Suffice that Reason keep to Nature's road,
> Subject, compound them, follow her and God.
> Love, Hope, and Joy, fair pleasure's smiling train,
> Hate, Fear, and Grief, the family of pain;
> These mix'd with art, and to due bounds confin'd,
> Make and maintain the balance of the mind:
> The lights and shades, whose well accorded strife
> Gives all the strength and colour of our life.
>
> [*Essay on Man*, II, 111-123]

These lines are full of echoes of Ovid and of kindred passages, for example, "fight," *pugnabant*; "Nature . . . and God," *deus et natura*; the opposites in terms of emotions; "due bounds," *limitibus certis*; "the balance of the mind," *tellus ponderibus librata suis*; "well accorded strife," *discordia concors*. Man's task of producing a moral harmony in his mind could be helped by the example of Nature, who makes it possible for him to alter the qualities of fruits by grafting; thus man should graft virtue onto his ruling passion (161-202). But vice must first be distinguished from virtue as God distinguished light and darkness (203-216) — as the Argument of the Second Epistle says, *"The limits near, yet the things* separate *and* evident." Man, therefore, must be the creator of his own moral being, ordering his own Chaos. The eventual result will be the formation of a good society, described in another Creation passage (III, 283-302), when a godlike man has restored Nature's Light.

> 'Till jarring int'rests of themselves create
> Th'according music of a well-mix'd State.
>
> [293-294]

This will be when man understands that God and Nature have resolved the strife between self and society.

> Thus God and Nature link'd the gen'ral frame,
> And bade Self-love and Social be the same.
>
> [317-318]

In the meantime, however, man's efforts to order his nature will meet with varying results, well depicted in the many character sketches occurring in the poems written around the same time as the *Essay on Man*. In these sketches, a good deal of use is made of the cosmological mode. The *Epistle to Bathurst* provides two examples of cosmological characters, in deliberate contrast. The Man of Ross (249-274) is shown as godlike in almost every line. Like Christ, he heals the sick and gives food to the crowd; or perhaps "divides the weekly bread" is as near as Pope dared to go, by a slight alteration to the Lord's Prayer, to suggesting that the Man was like God the Father. Like Moses, he draws water from the rock. His affinities with the *opifex rerum* are many and worth enumerating. First, Pope says,

> Pleas'd Vaga echoes thro' her winding bounds,
> And rapid Severn hoarse applause resounds,
>
> [251-252]

or, the Man is in harmony with the Nature of his native country, the slow Wye (one of the "rivers whom their winding borders fence") and the fast Severn, which symbolize *concordia discors*. Then, he "hung with woods yon mountain's sultry brow," at once bidding trees increase to woods and tempering heat with coolness. His causeway that "parts the vale with shady rows" does the same, and creates a temperate zone (admittedly between hot and hot, not hot and cold). His "heaven-directed spire" recalls lines 85-86 of Book I of the *Metamorphoses* (though these lines were in fact written about Prometheus, not the *opifex*)

> os homini sublime dedit caelumque videre
> iussit et erectos ad sidera tollere vultus;

and he parted strife or suits, *lites diremit,*

> Is there a variance? enter but his door,
> Balk'd are the Courts, and contest is no more.

Even the seats that he provides for travelers may be a joking reference to Sandys's "he to their seats confin'd."

The deathbed portrait of the Duke of Buckingham, whose "useless thousands" contrast with the Man of Ross's five hundred a year, is more compressed and, some would say, more poetical.

> In the worst inn's worst room, with mat half-hung,
> The floors of plaister, and the walls of dung,
> On once a flock-bed, but repair'd with straw,
> With tape-ty'd curtains, never meant to draw,
> The George and Garter dangling from that bed
> Where tawdry yellow strove with dirty red,
> Great Villers lies — alas! how chang'd from him,
> That life of pleasure, and that soul of whim!
> Gallant and gay, in Cliveden's proud alcove,
> The bow'r of wanton Strewsbury and love;
> Or just as gay, at Council, in a ring
> Of mimick'd Statesmen, and their merry King.
> No Wit to flatter, left of all his store!
> No Fool to laugh at, which he valu'd more.
> There, Victor of his health, of fortune, friends,
> And fame; this lord of useless thousands ends.

> [299-314]

This description expresses more than poverty and shabbiness: it expresses, above all, things ineptly intended, things out of place, *akosmia.* The mat hangings only half cover the walls; the floor is plastered, leaving dung for the walls; the bed is repaired with the wrong material; the curtains were never meant to draw, which is the function of curtains. The Garter is the symbol of Buckingham's life and attainments, and it seems probable that the tawdry yellow is the George, or gold jewel, and the dirty red with which it is at "strife" is the bed hangings, or covers; or possibly the yellow and red are both part of the bed. In any case, the Order is involved

in disorder, a pictorial translation, possibly, of *kosmos akosmos* (which the Sibylline line predicted when men are dying, as Buckingham is). Only such a room, one feels, is suitable for the last scene of the man who was as gay in Council as with a noble wanton; who valued fools more than wit; who strove with his own health, fortune, friends, and fame. The physical *akosmia* embodies *dedecus et rerum indignitas*, or *vita flagitiosa*, to give Stephanus's translations of *akosmia* in its moral sense.

In the *Epistle to Dr. Arbuthnot*, Pope uses cosmological language of his father,

> Born to no Pride, inheriting no Strife,
> Nor marrying Discord in a Noble Wife,
>
> [392-393]

a couplet that seems to refer back to the three great characters occurring earlier in the epistle. Bufo was proud; Atticus had married a noble wife and found discord in marriage ("Addison," says Johnson, "has left behind him no encouragement for ambitious love"). This would leave the third, Sporus, as the one who inherited strife in his nature: thus he is at once (*corpore in uno*) male and female, painted and dirty, and so on. His "buzz the witty and the fair annoys," that is, his discordant personality (we shall meet buzzing again), is in opposition to *nous*, or "mind," and to *kosmos*. He cannot balance his own mind, which resembles instead the most unbalanced thing there is, a seesaw, changing rapidly from one opposite to the other, now high, now low. At once cherub and reptile, with creeping wit and abased pride, he is the embodiment of the antithetical expression *kosmos akosmos*, which could, indeed, be translated by "beauty that shocks you." In this portrait Pope makes *akosmia* more evil than anywhere else and even associates it with Satan himself. Pope's own father, on the other hand, is a good man, lacking strife and discord, and avoiding lawsuits (*lites*). It seems possible that in one or two respects he is intended to recall Manilius's description of the cosmos: thus he "walked through his age" ("Its Course it urges on") and was healthy, though long-lived ("it keeps its Frame" and "no Years can waste" it).

Pope's opening note to the *Epistle to a Lady* leaves little
doubt that women too are dominated by *akosmia*: "Their particular characters are not so strongly mark'd as those of Men, seldom
so fixed, and still more inconsistent with themselves." The same
had already been implied in the *Rape of the Lock*.

> With varying Vanities, from ev'ry Part,
> They shift the moving Toyshop of their Heart;
> Where Wigs with Wigs, with Sword-knots Sword-knots strive,
> Beaus banish Beaus, and Coaches Coaches drive,
>
> [I, 99-102]

lines that suggest the instability and turmoil (note "strive") of
Chaos where *obstabat aliis aliud* (*Metamorphoses*, I, 17), or "All
were confus'd, and each disturb'd the rest" (Dryden's translation).
The reason for this state of affairs is presumably to be sought in
Heaven's alarmingly chancy manner of creating them, for the ingredients are shaken together rather than carefully arranged (*To a
Lady*, 280). With Martha Blount the result is happy, though even
she is a contradiction, for in her the opposite qualities are balanced — compare "Oh! blest with Temper" (257) with Ovid's
temperiemque dedit (*Metamorphoses*, I, 51). However, she is ex-
ceptional, and most women are continually changing (*nulli sua
forma manebat*) and have discordant characters. No wonder then
that the artist must rely on chance effects to "trick off" woman.

> Pictures like these, dear Madam, to design,
> Asks no firm hand, and no unerring line;
> Some wand'ring touch, or some reflected light,
> Some flying stroke alone can hit 'em right:
> For how should equal Colours do the knack?
>
> [151-155]

The "unerring line" that is not needed would translate *limes certus*, and the vulgar phrase "do the knack" well expresses the Epicurean carelessness of the approach.

Pope's cosmological treatment of women's characters is on
the whole not schematic, apart from this one playful example:

> Papillia, wedded to her doating spark,
> Sighs for the shades — "How charming is a Park!"
> A Park is purchased, but the Fair he sees
> All bath'd in tears — "Oh odious, odious Trees!"
>
> [37-40]

Here we see the four elements in turmoil (Papillia's sighs represent air, and her own name recalls the airy butterfly; the park is land or earth). We notice that "the Fair" suggests *kosmos* and that Papillia does not "bid trees increase to woods." All these allusions are signs of her ill-balanced nature.

Except for Cloe, who lacks all life, all those in the early part of the epistle are at strife with themselves, like Narcissa, in whom the opposites are not reconciled, "Now Conscience chills her, and now Passion burns" (65), or the ill-balanced Silia, "Sudden, she storms! she raves!" (33), or Calypso, who just avoids the antitheses of both *kosmos* and *nous*, "Was just not ugly, and was just not mad" (50), and yet "creates" passion. The most impressive and strifeful of the characters is Atossa,

> Who, with herself, or others, from her birth
> Finds all her life one warfare upon earth;
>
> [117-118]

she is an amalgam of wisdom and folly, hate and love. Yet, as with Timon, we are reminded at the end that she is part of the larger cosmos and that her extreme wealth may be destined to temper poverty.

V

Earlier in this study, the attempt was made to show that *Windsor Forest* and, on a smaller scale, the description of Timon's villa are both constructed on the cosmic model of the *Metamorphoses*. It will be contended now that Pope's two mock epics, the *Rape of the Lock* and the *Dunciad*, are at the same time cosmo-

logical, or mock-cosmological, poems. This is less easy to perceive with the *Rape of the Lock*, which has a strong narrative line
of more or less everyday happenings and whose cosmological passages are more heavily disguised; nevertheless, the pattern is there.

Since the poem has borne various interpretations, some conflicting, I shall here outline the one that seems to fit best with its
cosmological aspect and that I believe to be correct. It is a poem
about trivialities taken seriously, the mistake that, in the words of
Pope's dedication, "many modern ladies" fall into — "Let an action be never so trivial in itself, they always make it appear of the
utmost importance." The actions in the poem are indeed trivial in
themselves, including the two that so greatly stir Belinda, her win
at ombre and her loss of her lock. The ombre is played merely to
while away a few minutes, and it is played without stakes, which
might have given the game some real significance, especially if
Belinda had compromised herself, or had come near to doing so,
by accepting money to cover a loss. The loss of hairs is customar-
ily trivial, and what happens to hair once cut cannot matter to a
sensible person. We must therefore take Pope's endless sugges-
tions that the hair is of the utmost importance, some conveyed
with the greatest subtlety in allusions to Homer, Virgil, Milton,
and other illustrious voices of the past, as mere irony, that mocks
the feminine aptitude to magnify and forms "the kind of writing
very like tickling," to quote his own description for the poem.

Since the *Rape of the Lock* is constructed on the classical epic
model, the main theme is announced at the very beginning, and it
is noticeable that we can interpret the opening couplet in terms of
Pope's cosmology. The first line tells us of strife prevailing over
and displacing love and the second, of strife arising from judging
ill, for a person of good judgment would not permit trivial
things to give rise to mighty contests but would rather seek to
settle contests, *dirimere lites*. Pope makes the themes of triviality,
strife, and judging ill pervade the whole poem. His use of zeugmas — honor and brocade, counsel and tea, and so on — is famous. In the past they seem to have been seen merely as a pleasan-
try, but some modern critics perceive that they are a means of

satirizing the false values of society. It is of interest that Pope himself despised zeugmas, for in a note on the Iliad ix 648 he says, "We may indeed meet with such little Affectations in *Ovid*, — *Aurigam pariter animaque, rotisque, Expulit* — and the like; but the Taste of the Ancients in general was too good for these Fooleries." However, zeugmas have a cosmological significance, for they are nothing other than things ill joined, an artistic disorder that Pope admitted to reflect the *kosmos akosmos* of the poem.

A picture of a disordered society is given also by these well-known lines from near the beginning of Canto III:

> Mean while declining from the Noon of Day,
> The Sun obliquely shoots his burning Ray;
> The hungry Judges soon the Sentence sign,
> And Wretches hang that Jury-men may Dine;
> The Merchant from th' *Exchange* returns in Peace,
> And the long Labours of the *Toilette* cease.
>
> [19-23]

The first couplet tells us that it is early afternoon. The second couplet, much discussed, is an echo of lines in the Odyssey which Fenton later translated

> What-time the Judge forsakes the noisy bar
> To take repast, and stills the wordy war.
>
> [XII, 439-440]

Pope has adapted Homer to show the misperformance of the act of judgement: the most solemn decision is made for the most absurdly petty of reasons, that the judge and jury want their food. Again, this is the place in Homer where the phrase *krinein neikea* occurs, which, as we have seen, Stephanus refers to and translates *dirimere lites*: this reminds us that judging is akin to creation, since "*hanc deus et melior litem natura diremit;*" hence, this piece of "judging ill" is a sign of *akosmia*. The third couplet shows us things happening at the wrong time. The merchant leaves work when the time for it has only half passed, for, as Psalm 104, that great poem of God's ordered Creation (which shows affinities

with the Creation story in both Genesis and the *Metamorphoses*), has it, "Man goeth forth unto his work and to his labour until the evening"; or, in Sandys's paraphrase, which may be worth quoting since Pope admired his versification,

> Men with the Morning rise, to Labour prest,
> Toil all the Day, at Night return to rest.

The toilet, on the other hand, should have been a fairly brief task and should have been finished long before. So here again we see a *kosmos akosmos* and disorder caused by trivial things.

The first event in the poem to be described as cosmological is Belinda's creating of her own appearance. The scene plays on the same senses of *kosmos* as the story of Lodona in *Windsor Forest*: order, beauty, and feminine adornment, or *mundus muliebris*.[8] In adoring the "cosmetic" powers, Belinda seeks to become at least *ornandi perita*, in the words of Stephanus's definition of *kosmēti-kos*, and probably *ordinandi perita* also, since we see both order and variety in her dressing room. Betty and Belinda's "curious toil" echoes the "prudent care" with which the *opifex rerum* had unfolded the elements; and the elements indeed appear in the following lines:

> This casket *India*'s glowing gems unlocks,
> And all *Arabia* breathes from yonder Box.
> . . . .
> Sees by Degrees a purer Blush arise,
> And keener Lightnings quicken in her Eyes
> [133-134, 143-144]

Water is represented by the blush, for as Sandys says, "Blushing is a resort of the blood to the face" (p. 361), and blood is a liquid like water; and Sandys compares rivers to "blood in the veins" in his note on the new-created globe. We may especially note, among other cosmological indications that the reader will probably find easily enough, a lurking *akosmia* of things ill joined in the famous line "Puffs, Powders, Patches, Bibles, Billet-doux," for Be-

linda's is a frivolous and precarious creation of an appearance only, not of anything more real.

The *akosmia* of Belinda's nature is revealed by her inclination toward strife at the card table. She burns for the contest and is moved by a "thirst of fame" similar to the "thirst of glory" which Sandys, in a note on page 189 dealing with Ovid's account of the Muses in Book V of the *Metamorphoses*, makes a characteristic of Mars, the god of strife. She shows skill and care in reviewing her force, and as trumps she chooses spades, which are in fact swords (Italian: *spade*); if she had been inclined to love, she might have chosen hearts. Her raucous behavior upon winning shows that the balance of her mind is easily upset and points forward to her even more unbalanced behavior when she loses her lock. A hint of her character may have been suggested by the lack of metrical variety and balance in the lines that describe her in the barge, lines attacked by romantic critics hostile to Pope. The Baron too is inclined to strife; notice that his trophies, three garters and half a pair of gloves, are broken pairs whose very essence requires them to be joined. The "force and fraud" that he relies on are called the "cardinal virtues in war" in the famous thirteenth chapter of *Leviathan*, where society is described as a war of every man against every man; as a materialist, Hobbes belonged to the same party as Epicurus. Later we hear of the Baron's interest in stratagems and spoils, which Shakespeare tells us are the marks of a man without music in his soul. Probably, however, there is some irony in the description of the Baron, and he is shown as seen by Belinda and Thalestris, who exaggerate trifles, whereas to Clarissa's better judgment he is acceptable. Three garters and a glove seem rather meager trophies for a real amorist.

When the game is over, coffee is made:

> For lo! the Board with Cups and Spoons is crown'd,
> The Berries crackle, and the Mill turns round.
> On shining Altars of *Japan* they raise
> The silver Lamp; the fiery Spirits blaze.
> From silver Spouts the grateful Liquors glide,
> While *China*'s Earth receives the smoking Tyde.
> [III, 105-110]

The four elements show that this is a creation passage. Fire and water are obvious, and Pope has carefully named earth, leaving us to find air in "smoking" and perhaps in the "vapours" and "steams" which he mentions in the lines that follow. Possibly the circular motion of the mill is meant to carry a cosmological suggestion and even a reminiscence of Sandys's words "he turn'd it round," though in a different sense. As elsewhere in the poem, there seem to be signs of *akosmia*. The berries make a discordant crackling; and the shiny silver lamp is placed on shiny lacquer that, if imported from the Orient as Pope's words seem to mean (and must mean when he speaks of the porcelain), would have been black, thereby giving a stark juxtaposition of opposites rather than shades that "blend, soften, and unite." Thus the description may be intended as a criticism of the society that makes a ritual (note "altars") of coffee. Furthermore, the coffee is discordant in its effects, for it inspires the Baron's strategem to gain the prize and distracts Belinda's attention as he cuts.

The cutting of the lock is described in terms that, knowing Pope's cosmological language, we can see to be full of allusion.

> The Peer now spreads the glitt'ring *Forfex* wide
> T"inclose the Lock; now joins it, to divide.
>
> [III, 147 148]

Joining to divide is more than a verbal paradox when we think of the "unitive" Empedoclean love and the "discretive" strife. The scissors are ill joined indeed, for they not only cut Belinda's lock but also destroy the precarious order created at her dressing table. Belinda, who had been driven to one extreme by the triviality of her win at cards, is driven to the other by this trivial loss. Discordant screams follow, arising from rage and other violent emotions. Chaos is expressly invoked by Thalestris, who associates the disorder of social things out of place with that of cosmic things:

> Sooner shall Grass in *Hide*-Park *Circus* grow,
> And Wits take Lodgings in the Sound of *Bow*;
> Sooner let Earth, Air, Sea to *Chaos* fall,
> Men, Monkies, Lap-dogs, Parrots, perish all!
>
> [IV, 117-120]

In her speech lamenting the loss of her lock, Belinda asks,

> What mov'd my Mind with youthful Lords to rome?
> O had I stay'd, and said my Pray'rs at home!
>
> [IV, 159-160]

It may not be entirely fanciful to see here a recognition that she has broken harmony with God and left her appointed place, and for the reader to be reminded here of Dryden's Ovid,

> Thus disembroil'd, they take their proper place;
> The next of Kin contiguously embrace;
> And Foes are sunder'd by a larger space.
>
> [29-31]

Clarissa's appeal for good sense (*nous*) and good humor (*temperies*) is in vain, and the brawl begins. Pope seems to say that it stands for Chaos by showing the elements in conflict:

> *Jove*'s Thunder roars, Heav'n trembles all around;
> Blue *Neptune* storms, the bellowing Deeps resound;
> *Earth* shakes her nodding Tow'rs, the Ground gives way;
> And the pale Ghosts start at the Flash of Day.
>
> [V, 49-52]

If the flash represents fire, as it surely must, we have one line here for each element — air, water, earth and fire. All four appear again when Belinda conquers the Baron.

> See fierce *Belinda* on the *Baron* flies,
> With more than usual Lightning in her Eyes;
>
> . . . .
> Just where the Breath of Life his Nostrils drew,
> A Charge of *Snuff* the wily Virgin threw;
> The *Gnomes* direct, to ev'ry Atome just,
> The pungent Grains of titillating Dust.
> Sudden, with starting Tears each Eye o'erflows,
> And the high Dome re-ecchoes to his Nose.
>
> [V, 75-76, 81-86]

Here lightning is fire; breath is air; the snuff, called dust, and

directed by the earthy gnomes, is earth; and the tears are water. But *"hanc deus et melior litem natura diremit,"* by the metamorphosis of the lock into a star, which brings the strife to an end. The poet's prophecies explain the meaning of the miracle.

> This the *Beau-monde* shall from the *Mall* survey,
> And hail with Musick its propitious Ray;
>
> [V, 133-134]

That is, Society (*beau,* beauty, *kosmos; monde, mundus, kosmos*) will be at harmony (music, or *concordia discors*) with the universe, represented now by the lock as a sign of peace. Then again,

> This, the blest Lover shall for *Venus* take,
> And send up Vows from *Rosamonda*'s Lake;
>
> [V, 135-136]

that is, the lock is no longer a cause of strife, but a sign of love. Only the deluded Partridge, a furious Williamite, will see it as a sign of war, threatening ruin to France and Rome. Indeed, the reference to Partridge, and the fact that the metamorphosis of the lock alludes to Ovid's last metamorphosis, that of Julius Caesar's soul into a star that heralded the *Pax Augusta*, could almost persuade readers that that amiable dunce Esdras Barnivelt was not utterly wrong in his *Key to the Lock* and that the *Rape of the Lock* is (though in its way, not his) an allegory of the Peace of Utrecht.

Thus Belinda is left with an abstract and metaphysical consolation for the loss of her lock but has lost the chance of marrying the earthly lover who had found his way into her heart. Defying Clarissa's appeal, she has scorned a man and allowed strife to prevail, and so she has failed to pay due respect to the cosmic harmonies. We may recall Sherburne's translation of Manilius's lines on *discordia concors,*

> which kind Discordancy
> The Matrimonial Bands of Nature knits,
> And Principles for all Production fits,
>
> [I, 142-144; p. 13]

and his note, "This admirable Consent of the contrary Elements is here not unaptly called *The Matrimonial Band of Nature*. And for this reason . . . The Marriages of the Antients were confirmed and plighted by the Sacrament of two contrary Elements, Fire and Water."

When first published in 1714, the enlarged *Rape of the Lock* did not, of course, include Clarissa's speech and its explicit warning; yet there was perhaps no very great lacuna since Clarissa in fact repeats a subtler warning that Belinda should have drawn from the card table. In Pope's narrative within a narrative we are shown the destruction of an Epicurean world — Epicurean, because in cards, as in Milton's Chaos, chance, which Pope mentions twice, governs all and will destroy the world it has built. It is indeed a court world very like Belinda's own that we see at the begining of the hand, arranged by suit and rank in three bands each of the "sacred nine" (which Sandys in his note on the Muses already quoted rather cryptically calls "the triple trine which flows from the perfection of number"). It is an apparently orderly world, and Pope seems to emphasize the union of opposites in its composition: the majesty and age of the kings, the softness of the queens, the youth of the knaves, the blending of the parti-colored troops into "a shining train" (III, 37-44). However, there are signs of *akosmia* in it, for example, the "giant limbs" and "unwieldy state" of the king of clubs, with his pompous robe trailing behind. Belinda's "Let Spades be Trumps" is the signal for strife to begin; it is the reverse of Anne's "Let Discord cease" in *Windsor Forest*; it is spoken to start a war, not to conclude one. The early tricks are played in orderly fashion; the defeated cards are taken prisoner, not slain, and the victors march off the field; but the strife becomes ever fiercer as the cards give way to their own rage, pride, lust, and revenge. The slaughter at the end is described in cosmological language: they are now in "wild disorder," "dis-united" (or ill joined), falling in heaps (or *indigestae moles*), and distempered (reversing *temperiemque dedit*). But the lesson is lost on Belinda, who gives way to her own feelings and oversteps the social limits, rather as Lodona, too eager for the chase, had strayed beyond the forest limits.

The cosmological plan of the *Dunciad* is extremely simple and is essentially the same as that of the lines on Timon's villa. After the theogony of Dulness, the world is created; then actions suitable to its nature take place in it; then it is swept away. The scale, subject, and tone of the poem elicit from Pope a wider range of cosmological references than usual.

First Dulness is born to Chaos and Night; Pope's note points out that in Hesiod's *Theogony* Chaos had been "the Progenitor of all the Gods." Then, in the lines that follow, Dulness creates the world of the poem.

> Here she beholds the Chaos dark and deep,
> Where nameless Somethings in their causes sleep,
> 'Till genial Jacob, or a warm Third day,
> Call forth each mass, a Poem, or a Play:
> How hints, like spawn, scarce quick in embryo lie,
> How new-born nonsense first is taught to cry,
> Maggots half-form'd in rhyme exactly meet,
> And learn to crawl upon poetic feet.
> Here one poor word an hundred clenches makes,
> And ductile dulness new meanders takes;
> There motley Images her fancy strike,
> Figures ill pair'd, and Similies unlike.
> She sees a Mob of Metaphors advance,
> Pleas'd with the madness of the mazy dance:
> How Tragedy and Comedy embrace;
> How Farce and Epic get a jumbled race;
> How Time himself stands still at her command,
> Realms shift their place, and Ocean turns to land.
> Here gay Description Ægypt glads with show'rs,
> Or gives to Zembla fruits, to Barca flow'rs;
> Glitt'ring with ice here hoary hills are seen,
> There painted vallies of eternal green,
> In cold December fragrant chaplets blow,
> And heavy harvests nod beneath the snow.
>
> [I, 55-78]

Here is the *rudis indigestaque moles* in literary form, and even when the act of Creation is complete, it is still only a wild (*indi-*

gestus) creation, or *kosmos akosmos. Akosmia* is expressed in things ill joined (only the maggots are well joined — better if not), things out of place, and things contradictory in their essence, such as similes unlike. The same elements of ineptitude which compose the universe will compose the souls of the dunces that inhabit it, predestining them to folly, humbug, and dullness which can end only with the end of the universe — not that that is long in coming. These themes are echoed in a second Creation passage (III, 231-248), that describing Rich's pantomimes, in which "a new world to Nature's laws unknown" (that is, *kosmos akosmos*) is born.

There are various echoes and parodies of the Creation themes that we have been examining. For example, Dulness parts the strife, *dirimit litem*, of Dennis and Gildon:

> Blockheads with reason wicked wits abhor,
> But fool with fool is barb'rous civil war.
> Embrace, embrace my sons!
>
> [III, 175-177]

Again, Cibber yearns to be orderly disposed by *limites certi*:

> Secure us kindly in our native night.
> Or, if to Wit a coxcomb make pretence,
> Guard the sure barrier between that and Sense.
>
> [I, 176-178]

Then when Dulness creates in the Lucretian way, by a lucky hit, a poet's form for the booksellers to run for, "senseless, lifeless! idol void and vain!" (II, 46), it is surely a parody of line 76 of Ovid's first book *"sanctius his animal, mentisque capacius altae."* Again, the polluted Thames of the diving contest distorts the crystal Thames of *Windsor Forest* and its beautiful tributary streams.

However, what seems to be Pope's chief resource in conveying the chaotic character of the *Dunciad* world is to infuse the poem with themes and images drawn from Ovid's description of Chaos itself, and particularly from these lines:

unus erat toto naturae vultus in orbe,
quem dixere chaos: rudis indigestaque moles
nec quicquam nisi pondus iners, congestaque eodem
non bene iunctarum discordia semina rerum.
. . . .
. . . nulli sua forma manebat.

[6-9, 17]

("Nature had one countenance in all the world, which men have called Chaos: a rough, unordered mass, nothing but an inert weight and the discordant atoms, packed together, of things ill-joined. . . . Nothing kept its shape.")

There are many things ill joined in the *Dunciad*, though they are not perhaps so conspicuous as in the *Rape of the Lock*: miscellanies (I, 39); Hockley-hole and White's, dukes and butchers (I, 220-221); morning prayer and flagellation (II, 270); *Pluto* and *Cato*, *The Mourning Bride* and *Proserpine* (III, 309-310); Milton and Johnston (IV, 112); a nest, a toad, a fungus, and a flower (IV, 400); and a fire, a jig, a battle, and a ball (III, 239). The florist even boasts, with unconscious irony, of light ill joined in *akosmia*:

Did Nature's pencil ever blend such rays,
Such vary'd light in one promiscuous blaze?
[IV, 411-412]

Things ill joined will produce discord and the strife of Chaos, the discretive or divisive force of Empedocles' theory, celebrated by the form of Italian opera, "Joy to great Chaos! let Division reign" (IV, 54), who herself joins joy, grief, and rage. There is discord in the noise contest, indeed the games as a whole are a form of strife, degrading and destroying the creations of art. The warfare of Dulness on art is symbolized by the barbarian invasions and the Mohammedan conquests.

See the bold Ostrogoths on Latium fall;
See the fierce Visigoths on Spain and Gaul!
See, where the morning gilds the palmy shore

(The soil that arts and infant letters bore)
His conqu'ring tribes th' Arabian prophet draws.

[III, 93-97]

The pedagogues and pedants war on spirit and soul by violence
with the birch, like Busby (IV, 139 ff.); by expulsion (IV, 196); and
by division, which reduces literature to particles and even letters
and so destroys the harmony of the creation (IV, 209 ff., 235-236).

Chaos was heavy, *nec quicquam nisi pondus iners*, and there
is no commoner image in the *Dunciad* than that of lifeless weight.
Dulness herself is heavy (I, 15; III, 295), and her kingdom is to be
an age of lead (I, 28; IV, 27). Cibber's head is like a ponderous bowl
(which, incidentally, is biased and not *ponderibus librata suis*);
his inspiration is compared to the force that moves leaden slugs
and to clock weights (I, 180–184); the weight of his books makes
the shelves groan (I, 154). The mock poet is an immovable bulk
(II, 39); the quality Dulness values in authors is heaviness (II, 368);
Arnall's skull is ponderous (II, 315), solidified no doubt by Bavius
(III, 25–26). The books read in the soporific contest are ponderous
(III, 383, 388); Gilbert the soporific preacher is leaden (IV, 608);
the first prize in the diving contest is lead, the second, coals (II,
281). The pedagogues load the mind with chains and padlocks
(IV, 157 ff.). *Pondus iners*, stated or implied, permeates the whole
poem.

Weight, of course, is a property of matter, and it seems that in
the *Dunciad*, and especially in Book IV, Pope adopts the Stoic
opinion expressed by Sandys in his opening note on Chaos: "God
they held to be the Minde, and *Chaos* the Matter." The force of
Dulness is *vis inertiae* (IV, 7), which, as the note explains, is "the
Foundation of all the Qualities and Attributes of that sluggish
substance" (that is, matter). Two or three times, in the text and the
notes, Pope refers to Epicureanism, the materialist philosophy.
Thus the note on Book IV, line 15 explains the "Epicurean opinion, that from the Dissolution of the natural World into Night
and Chaos, a new one should arise";[9] that on Book IV, line 494

gives the Epicurean origin of "seeds of fire," the divinity of the pedants is mindless, a contradiction in terms (IV, 244); the gloomy clerk seeks to bind God in matter, and would prefer an Epicurean God (IV, 476, 484).

Chaos is ever shifting and changing its shape, *nulli sua forma manebat*, and the *Dunciad* reflects this attribute in many illusions and metamorphoses. The universe of Dulness (I, 55 ff.) is one in which the literary kinds are broken and transformed and in which "Realms shift their place, and Ocean turns to land." The mock world of Rich's pantomine is completely turned into a new one (III, 235 ff.). Bards, like Proteus, turn to monsters (I, 38); Cibber's soul changes its earthly habitation (III, 49); the Duke of Kingston turns to air (IV, 322). Dulness turns prose to verse, and she and the pedants turn verse to prose (I, 274; IV, 214). The mock poet deludes the booksellers by vanishing to air (II, 109 ff.); conceit and interest delude by changing or casting false light upon their dupes' appearance (IV, 532 ff.), Chi Ho-am-ti turns learning to air (III, 78); Ripley transforms the London of Jones, Wren, and Burlington (III, 327 ff.).

Another master image of the *Dunciad* is that of the crowd, of things *congesta eodem*. The crowd unites the characteristics of Chaos: it is ill joined, strifeful, dense, mindless, and variable. The poem is crowded from the very beginning by the productions of the dunces: elegiacs, journals, medleys, merc'ries, magazines, epitaphs, and odes (I, 42 ff.). The Creation passage is packed with hints, nonsense, clenches by the hundred, motley images, a mob of metaphors, "all these, and more." Cibber's floor is crowded with embryo and abortion, his shelves with endless volumes. Dulness promises him the escort of an army of dunces (I, 306), and at the beginning of Book II he is surrounded by a company of them as new crowds are summoned.

> An endless band
> Pours forth, and leaves unpeopled half the land.
> A motley mixture! in long wigs, in bags,
> In silks, in crapes, in Garters, and in rags,
> From drawing rooms, from colleges, from garrets,

On horse, on foot, in hacks, and gilded chariots:
All who true Dunces in her cause appear'd,
And all who knew those Dunces to reward.

[II, 19-26]

There are the spectators of the games, and sometimes too the participants form a crowd,

Now thousand tongues are heard in one loud din:
The Monkey-mimics rush discordant in;
'Twas chatt'ring, grinning, mouthing, jabb'ring all,
[II, 235-237]

and "Next plung'd a feeble, but a desp'rate pack" (II, 305). As the crowd swells and spreads, it becomes more chaotic; dark (*lucis egens aer*) and full of strife,

Around him wide a sable Army stand,
A low-born, cell-bred, selfish, servile band,
Prompt or to guard or stab, to saint or damn,
Heav'n's Swiss, who fight for any God, or Man.
    Thro' Lud's fam'd gates, along the well-known Fleet
Rolls the black troop, and overshades the street.

[II, 355-360]

This crowd is only a portion of the vast mass of dunces, some waiting to be born,

Millions and millions on these banks he views,
Thick as the stars of night, or morning dews,
[III, 31-32]

others already active in the world,

from Hyperborean skies
Embody'd dark, what clouds of Vandals rise!
Lo! where Mæotis sleeps, and hardly flows
The freezing Tanais thro' a waste of snows,
The North by myriads pours her mighty sons.

[III, 85-89]

England too had been crowded by

> Men bearded, bald, cowl'd, uncowl'd, shod, unshod,
> Peel'd, patch'd, and pyebald, linsey-wolsey brothers,
> Grave Mummers! sleeveless some, and shirtless others.
>
> [III, 114-116]

and will be again, by Dulness's allies,

> What aids, what armies to assert her cause!
> See all her progeny, illustrious sight!
> . . . .
> Each Songster, Riddler, ev'ry nameless name,
> All crowd.
>
> [III, 128-129, 157-158]

In Book IV the process is intensified; Fame summons all the nations:

> The young, the old, who feel her inward sway,
> One instinct seizes, and transports away.
> None need a guide, by sure Attraction led,
> And strong impulsive gravity of Head.
> None want a place, for all their Centre found,
> Hung to the Goddess, and coher'd around.
> Not closer, orb in orb, conglob'd are seen
> The buzzing Bees about their dusky Queen.
>   The gath'ring number, as it moves along
> Involves a vast involuntary throng,
> Who gently drawn, and struggling less and less,
> Roll in her Vortex, and her pow'r confess.
>
> [IV, 73-84]

Later the darkness of the crowd is further emphasized:

> Prompt at the call, around the Goddess roll
> Broad hats, and hoods, and caps, a sable shoal:
> Thick and more thick the black blockade extends,
> A hundred head of Aristotle's friends.
>
> [IV, 189-192]

The crowd is moved down the great chain of being, to bees and "locusts blackening all the ground" (IV, 397), a swarm with only one mind and will within it, the mind and will of Dulness, which act on the crowd as on mere matter. The couplet comparing the members of the crowd to bees,

> Not closer, orb in orb, conglob'd are seen
> The buzzing Bees about their dusky Queen,
>
> [IV, 79-80]

ought to be read together with Ovid,

> unus erat toto naturae vultus in orbe,
> quem dixere chaos: rudis indigestaque moles,
> nec quicquam nisi pondus iners, congestaque eodem
> non bene iunctarum discordia semina rerum.

Pope's lines, surely, are a conscious imitation. The buzzing bees are like the *discordia semina*, conglobed, or *congesta*, about their queen or center, *eodem*. In short, the dunces are a fragment of Chaos and will restore the time when

> unus erat toto naturae vultus in orbe,
> quem dixere chaos.

This was prophesied by Settle to Cibber when he showed him how extensive the conquests of Dulness were already,

> How little, mark! that portion of the ball,
> Where, faint at best, the beams of Science fall,
>
> [III, 83-84]

soon to be extinguished by the barbarians.

The poem and the universe end with the Yawn of Dulness, which comes at the climax of her speech. Everybody goes to sleep, then there is a gap marked by a row of asterisks, then the fifteen couplets of the conclusion, which is a reversed Creation passage. The events are rapid, and more strictly linked in cause and effect

than may appear; for Pope is here playing on "chaos" and its cognates in the same way as we have elsewhere seen him playing on *kosmos*. The yawn itself is the first sense, for as Stephanus and others make clear, "chaos" is derived from *khainein*, "to yawn," and its primary meaning is a gaping mouth, like a crocodile's. The asterisks mark a "chasm" in the text, and that too is cognate. Then, at the end, Chaos returns. The whole passage has a Hesiodic flavor. In a note at the beginning of the poem Pope reminds us that in the *Theogony* Chaos was the progenitor of all the gods, and here at the end he recalls the dark chasm of Tartarus in the *Theogony*.

There is more to all this, of course, than etymology and allusion: the Yawn represents a failure of mind, and when mind fails the universe is destroyed. The point is made in a passage of the *Astronomica* which has provided one model for the last line of the Dunciad (II, 67, p. 51):

> For did not all the Friendly Parts conspire
> To make one Whole, and keep the Frame intire;
> And did not Reason guide, and Sense controul
> The vast stupendous Machine of the Whole,
> *Earth* would not keep its place, the *Skies* would fall,
> And universal Stiffness deaden All.[10]

[II, 67-71; p. 52]

VI

Pope also employs the cosmological mode and the Creation theme in those poems that are written in the first person and which, in some degree at least, are autobiographical: the *Temple of Fame* among his earlier works and the *Imitations of Horace*. In the *Temple of Fame*, it is true, the narrator is very much a conventional lay figure, yet his circumstances reflect those of Pope, who, when he wrote it, knew, or could reasonably hope, that his own niche was reserved for him. The poem expresses, partly by cosmo-

logical means, his awareness that Fame is capricious, vulnerable to malice and fashion, and hardly to be distinguished from rumor and falsehood. At the opening his dreams arise in "wild order" (a phrase that was borrowed from Dryden, as the Twickenham note points out, and could be literally translated *kosmos akosmos*) but then "join" to compose an intellectual scene that seems to symbolize the achievements of the human mind in a landscape of ideal *concordia discors*.

> I stood, methought, betwixt Earth, Seas, and Skies,
> The whole Creation open to my Eyes:
> In Air self-ballanc'd hung the Globe below,
> Where Mountains rise, and circling Oceans flow;
> Here naked Rocks, and empty Wastes were seen,
> There Tow'ry Cities, and the Forests green;
> Here sailing Ships delight the wand'ring Eyes;
> There Trees, and intermingl'd Temples rise:
> Now a clear Sun the shining Scene displays,
> The transient Landscape now in Clouds decays.
>
> [11-20]

Here Pope cleverly adds the Ovidian touch of the self-balanced earth to his model from Chaucer's *Hous of Fame* (the passage is quoted in the Twickenham edition), so that other details also become Ovidianized; thus, the ships reverse Ovid's *innabilis unda* and the sunlight, his *lucis egens aer*. However, all is not as it seems from a distance, as Pope (if one may so call the narrator) discovers when he draws closer to the main feature of the landscape, the rock of ice surmounted by the Temple. On the lower parts of the rock names appear and disappear with disconcerting rapidity, and only the upper parts are secure; at the same time the neighborhood is filled with a "wild promiscuous sound," a sign, probably, of discord. After a long description of the truly great, represented by statues in the Temple, Pope shows us the Goddess in her shrine, and here again there seems to be disproportion, disharmony, and change of shape (*nulli sua forma manebat*):

> These massie Columns in a Circle rise,
> O'er which a pompous Dome invades the Skies:

> Scarce to the Top I stretch'd my aking Sight,
> . . . .
> When on the *Goddess* first I cast my Sight,
> Scarce seem'd her Stature of a Cubit's height,
> But swell'd to larger Size, the more I gaz'd,
> Till to the Roof her tow'ring Front she rais'd.
>
> [244-246, 258-261]

There are other hints of *akosmia* in the description of the crowd that the Goddess summons, lines that Pope remembered in the *Dunciad*:

> And all the Nations, summon'd at the Call,
> From diff'rent Quarters fill the crowded Hall:
> Of various Tongues the mingled Sounds were heard;
> In various Garbs promiscuous Throngs appear'd;
> Thick as the Bees . . .
>
> [278-282]

The sound of her trumpet is uncertain, now sweet, now direful. Later, when the scene shifts to the Temple of Rumour, Pope stands on the brink of Chaos. This temple is unstable (*instabilis tellus*) and discordant,

> Its Site uncertain, if in Earth or Air;
> With rapid Motion turn'd the Mansion round;
> With ceaseless Noise the ringing Walls resound.
>
> [421-423]

The proceedings there are described in cosmological language:

> There various News I heard, of Love and Strife,
> Of Peace and War, Health, Sickness, Death, and Life;
> Of Loss and Gain, of Famine and of Store,
> Of Storms at Sea, and Travels on the Shore,
> Of Prodigies, and Portents seen in Air,
> Of Fire and Plagues, and Stars with blazing Hair,
> Of Turns of Fortune, Changes in the State,
> The Falls of Fav'rites, Projects of the Great,

Of old Mismanagements, Taxations new —
All neither wholly false, nor wholly true.

[447-457]

Here the opposites and the elements are shown in a turmoil of love and strife very like the original turmoil of Chaos. The opposites are peace, war; health, sickness; death, life; loss, gain; famine, store. The elements follow in order — water, earth, air, and fire in lines 451 to 453 (on the fieriness of plagues see *Essay on Man*, "From burning suns when livid deaths descend" [I, 142], and the Twickenham note). Affairs of state and the doings of politicians are most naturally assimilated into this strife, which is described in ever wilder terms, ending with truth and falsehood "contending for the way" (490 — *obstabatque aliis aliud*) and becoming ill joined (494–496). This is the world that Pope declines to enter.

In his later verse Pope appears as the *opifex rerum* of his own world, a position that he no doubt thought he had earned by his devotion to the principle of *concordia discors* in the arts and in life as he endeavored to

smooth and harmonize [his] mind
Teach ev'ry Thought within its bounds to roll,
[*Imitations of Horace: Epistles*, II, ii, 203-204]

like the rivers of Creation. In one of the most vivid and personal passages of the *Imitations of Horace* (*Satires*, II, i, 123), Pope shows us himself with his friends in the retreat of his grotto world at Twickenham, a world of art far different from "that world" of the city, diligently formed by the selection and blending of materials and provided with an allusion to their pristine chaotic state, to judge by the description left by his gardener John Searle: "At the entrance of the Grotto . . . are various sorts of stone thrown promiscuously together, like an old Ruine."[11]

Know, all the distant Din that World can keep
Rolls o'er my *Grotto*, and but sooths my Sleep.
There, my Retreat the best Companions grace,

> Chiefs, out of War, and Statesmen, out of Place.
> The *St. John* mingles with my friendly Bowl,
> The Feast of Reason and the Flow of Soul:
> And He, whose Lightning pierc'd th' *Iberian* Lines,
> Now, forms my Quincunx, and now ranks my Vines,
> Or tames the Genius of the stubborn Plain,
> Almost as quickly, as he conquer'd *Spain*.
>
> [123-132]

Bolingbroke is godlike because he provides two gifts, reason and
soul, bestowed on man at the Creation, and these are presented as
opposites, feast and flow, solid and liquid, which Bolingbroke
unites. The "friendly bowl" is almost certainly a symbol of the
Empedoclean *philotēs*. The phrase is in fact a literal translation
of *philotēsios kratēr*, meaning a "pledging-bowl," which Stephanus discusses at some length in the subarticle immediately
following that on *philotēs*. Peterbrough is godlike because he
wields the lightning, a divine power ("he, whose hand the lightning forms"), and orders nature by forming, ranking, and taming
her. Pope is the creator of the grotto and has united these two
opposite men in harmony (as in himself he unites the opposites of
the Cyrenaic Aristippus and St. Paul). Although they are out of
"their proper place" in the greater world, they can take their place
in Pope's world. The whole scene is a well-accorded microcosm,
the antithesis of Timon's villa.[12]

There is further Creation material in the *Imitations of Horace*, for example, in Pope's mockery of George II as godlike (*Epistles*, II, i) because he balances the world (2), parts strife, and har-
monizes the opposites (397 ff.). It seems unnecessary to expound
all such diffused references, but some passages must be pointed
out. First, we should examine the main link between Horace and
the cosmology represented by Ovid's Creation. The Horatian
ideal of the golden mean can naturally be understood as a moral
embodiment of *concordia discors*, for as in Aristotle's ethics,
which lie behind Horace, the virtues subsist as the means between
extreme vices, so the world is held in being by the balanced tension of the opposites. Horace, for example, pleads for the "tem-

perate use" of riches; Ovid points to the part played by temperance in the Creation of the world and of life, *"temperiemque dedit,"* and

> quippe ubi temperiem sumpsere umorque calorque
> concipiunt, et ab his oriuntur cuncta duobus.

The story of Phaethon illustrates the point. His driving is uncontrolled because he lacks self-restraint, and he is unwilling or unable to take his father's advice *medio tutissimus ibis (Metamorphoses*, II, 137). Sandys's translation of these words, "the safer Meane is best," is significantly similar to Stanley's remark on Aristotle's ethics, "the mean, relating to us, is in all the best." As a result, Phaethon threatens to bring about the literal end of the universe by the displacement of the ordered elements so that the earth cries *"in chaos antiquum confundimur"* (299). His story was taken by Sandys as the allegory of the rash prince who "gives no limits to his ruining ambition," whereas princes ought "to run a regular course . . . neither to incline to the right hand nor the left . . . the middle way being only safe" (pp. 66-67). As with the art of government, so with the whole art of life; and Pope versifies Sandys's words, themselves closely based on Ovid (II, 137-140), into a most Horatian-seeming couplet (*Satires*, II, ii):

> He knows to live, who keeps the middle state,
> And neither leans on this side, nor on that.
>
> [61-62]

In the same passage Pope equates intemperance with Chaos.

> The stomach (cram'd from ev'ry dish,
> A Tomb of boil'd, and roast, and flesh, and fish,
> Where Bile, and wind, and phlegm, and acid jar,
> And all the Man is one intestine war)
> Remembers oft the School-boy's simple fare,
> The temp'rate sleeps, and spirits light as air!
>
> [69-74]

Here is an indigested mass indeed: boiled and roast represent wa-

ter and fire, and flesh and fish probably earth and water; and the ingredients of line 71 certainly include water and air and perhaps fire (the burning acid) as well. While this intestine war (or perhaps dreadful series of intestine wars) rages, Creation cannot proceed to its culminating act,

> What life in all that ample Body say,
> What heav'nly Particle inspires the clay?
>
> [77-78]

Pope, on the other hand, knows how to create a balanced dinner, or *kosmein dorpon*, "to set a supper in order," in the Homeric phrase that Stephanus cites under *kosmos*. Here is one of the best hidden and humblest of Pope's Creation passages:

> 'Tis true, no Turbots dignify my boards,
> But gudgeons, flounders, what my Thames affords.
> To Hounslow-heath I point, and Bansted-down,
> Thence comes your mutton, and these chicks my own:
> From yon old wallnut-tree a show'r shall fall;
> And grapes, long-ling'ring on my only wall,
> And figs, from standard and Espalier join.
>
> [141-147]

Matthew Arnold took this for prose, but as Sandys says in his note on the Muses, already quoted:

> Verse hath a greater efficacy then prose: which penetrates deeper, and makes a more lasting impression. For as the voice passing through the narrow conduit of a trumpet breakes forth more cleare and musicall: even so the sence contracted by the strict necessity of numbers. The other is heard with more negligence, and lesse impulsion: but when the excellent matter is restrained in measures, the same sentence not only allures but inforceth. [p. 190]

Here the Thames, Pope's early symbol of *concordia discors*, provides the fish; and the mutton, he carefully tells us, comes from two pastures, the heath and the down, recalling

> Here in full Light the russet Plains extend;
> There wrapt in Clouds the blueish Hills ascend,
>
> [*Windsor Forest*, 23-24]

and "To him no high, no low" (*Essay-on Man*, I, 279). Perhaps also the fish, mutton and chicks represent the harmony of water, earth and air, being cooked (as the Shield of Achilles was forged) by the fourth element, fire. The walnuts and grapes embody at least three pairs of opposites, for the walnuts fall in a shower, sudden and swift, while the grapes are lingering and slow; and they are hard and soft, *mollia cum duris*, and dry and moist. Finally, the figs "join" from opposite tree-forms, one low and thin, one high and thick, but each shaped by Pope's art. Not to be satisfied with this agreeable feast is to be at odds with God and Nature, and so the conclusion follows "The dev'l is in you if you cannot dine" (148).

VII

It seems that Pope could hardly drink tea without thinking of the Creation. One reason for his passion for order may have been the great misfortune of his illness and the disorder of his body. His own story can be looked at in a cosmological way and seems to show a curious parallel with the stories of Lodona and Belinda. Lodona was too eager for the chase and so strayed outside the Forest limits to suffer violation by Pan, who, according to Sandys, represented "universal Nature." Readmitted to the Forest by the divine power of Diana, she remained there in altered form, unable to hunt any more or to take part in the Forest life but able to reflect the world to the inhabitants. Belinda's fall from dignity at the card table lost her the respect that her graceful ease in the barge had commanded, but a godlike poet was able to make her lock, at least, the cynosure of every eye again. Pope also offended, as he believed, by excess of study in childhood, or "perpetual application" as he put it to Spence, and destroyed the harmony of his microcosm, "the body's harmony"; but like the blind minstrel in the *Odyssey*, he had been given both good and evil and was able to regain concord of a kind and to reflect the world through his godlike art, a power akin to the universal love "who raised the heavy, illuminated the obscure, quickned the dead, gave forme to the deformed, and perfection to the imperfect: which was no other then

that harmony in nature created by the Almighties *Fiat*" — hence, perhaps, his insistence that unsatisfactory or disordered micro-cosms like Timon's villa would one day be reabsorbed into the cosmic order.

Such speculation may be vain, but the more we learn about Pope's language of allusion, which we can do through familiarity with his sources, the more we see how in every aspect of life he endlessly invokes God's design in nature, much as the propor-tions of an ideal Palladian building invoke the cosmic harmonies.

CHAPTER 4

Manilius, Creech, and "An Essay on Man"

I

An Essay on Man, one of the few sustainedly ratiocinative poems to have kept a place in living literature, has been called Stoicism in verse, but this description is only partly true. It is Stoic, nearly enough, in its view of God and the universe but at odds with Stoicism over the nature of man; in fact Pope has the reduction of man's "Stoic pride" as one of his chief aims. My purpose here is to show that there is a strong, though not a simple, relationship between the *Essay* and the *Astronomica* and that Pope used Manilius as a prime source of Stoic material, preferring him to other Stoic writers no doubt largely because of the existence of a translation in heroic couplets. Lucretius's doctrine was anathema to the age and, as we have seen, to Pope, but Manilius was in tune with modern thought as Creech pointed out in his preface:

> This *Manilius* . . . had a liberal Education suitable to his Quality and the time in which he liv'd: his Writings shew him to be well acquainted with the Principles of the several Sects of Philosophers, but addicted to the *Stoicks*, whose Hypothesis in all its out-lines bears a near resemblance to some of the Theories that are now in Fashion. The Modern Philosophers build Worlds according to the Models of the Antient Heathens, and *Zeno* is the Architect. [pp. 60-61]

105

Creech goes on to give a brief sketch of Stoicism:

> The Stoicks Principles were in short these: They say there is one
> Infinite, Eternal, Almighty Mind, which being diffus'd thro' the
> whole Universe of well order'd and regularly dispos'd Matter, ac-
> tuates every part of it, and is as it were, the Soul of this vast Body.
> . . . They farther add, that this Infinite Mind hath made one gen-
> eral decree concerning the Government of the lower World, and
> executes it by giving such and such Powers to the Celestial Bodies,
> as are sufficient and proper to produce the design'd Effects: This
> *Decree* thus executed they call *Fate*, and upon this Principle their
> whole System of *Astrology* depends: That some things happen'd in
> the World which were very unaccountable every days Experience
> taught them; they learn'd also or pretended to have learn'd from
> very many accurate, and often repeated Observations, that there
> was a constant Agreement between those odd unaccountable Acci-
> dents and such and such Positions of the Heavenly Bodies, and
> therefore concluded that those Bodies were concern'd in those Ef-
> fects. Hence they began to settle Rules, and to draw their scatter'd
> Observations into an Art. [pp. 61-63]

This extract epitomizes both what Pope accepted and what he
rejected in Stoicism.

The passage of the *Astronomica* which best expresses the
Stoic cosmology is probably the following, which Creech heads
"The World an Animal, and God the Soul of it."

> I'll sing how *God* the World's Almighty Mind
> Thro' *All* infus'd, and to that *All* confin'd,
> Directs the Parts, and with an equal Hand
> Supports the *whole*, enjoying his Command:
> How All agree, and how the Parts have made
> Strict Leagues, subsisting by each others Aid;
> How All by Reason move, because one Soul
> Lives in the Parts, diffusing thro' the whole.
>   For did not all the Friendly Parts conspire
> To make one Whole, and keep the Frame intire;
> And did not Reason guide, and Sense controul
> The vast stupendous Machine of the whole,

Earth would not keep its place, the *Skies* would fall,
And universal Stiffness deaden All;
Stars would not wheel their Round, nor *Day*, nor *Night*,
Their Course perform, be put, and put to flight:
Rains would not feed the Fields, and *Earth* deny
Mists to the *Clouds*, and Vapors to the *Sky*;
Seas would not fill the *Springs*, nor *Springs* return
Their grateful Tribute from their flowing Urn:
Nor would the *All*, unless contriv'd by Art,
So justly be proportion'd in each part,
That neither Seas, nor Skies, nor Stars exceed
Our Wants, nor are too scanty for our Need:
Thus stands the Frame, and the *Almighty* Soul
Thro' all diffus'd so turns, and guides the whole,
That nothing from its setled Station swerves,
And *Motion* alters not the Frame, but still preserves.

　　　　　　　　　　　　　[II, 60-80; pp. 51-52]

Here we may see germs of such passages as

　　　All are but parts of one stupendous whole,
　　Whose body, Nature is, and God the soul,
　　　　　　　　　[I, 267-268]

and of the cosmological lines from *To Bathurst,*

　　　That POW'R who bids the Ocean ebb and flow,
　　　Bids seed-time, harvest, equal course maintain,
　　　Thro' reconcil'd extremes of drought and rain,
　　　Builds Life on Death, on Change Duration founds,
　　　And gives th' eternal wheels to know their rounds.
　　　　　　　　　　　[166-170]

Pope used distortions of the same lines, also, in descriptions of
disorder, as in the passage beginning, "Let Earth, unbalanc'd,
from her orbit fly" and in the last line of the *Dunciad.*

　　It is worth noting that Pope does not carry his agreement
with Stoicism to the point of accepting that the world is itself
God, as in these lines from the *Astronomica:*

aut neque terra patrem novit nec flamma nec aer
aut umor, faciuntque deum per quattuor artus.

Or whether Water, Air, and Flame and Earth
Knew no beginning, no *first* seeds of Birth;
But first in Being from themselves arose,
And as four Members the vast *God* compose.
                    [I, 137-138; Creech's translation, p. 8]

Sandys had been censured by the orthodox for identifying God
with nature in his translation of Ovid's *deus et melior natura* and
in his notes, and Pope was anxious to avoid the same censure. As
Mack's Twickenham note points out, he was concerned that his
reference to God as the soul of the world should not be "taken for
heathenism," and so he wrote to his pious Catholic friend Caryll
when it was still unknown that the *Essay* was his (it was, of course,
first published anonymously) that the author was "quite Chris-
tian in his system." However, he did not save himself from much
pious dislike, often pretending to be literary criticism, in generations to come.

II

Yet although Pope seems broadly to accept the Stoic view of
God and the universe, he utterly rejects the Stoics' view of man as a
being having been endowed by God with all-powerful reason that
he could use to grasp God's entire purpose, a being on a plane far
above, and different in kind from, the rest of animate creation. It is
this aspect of Stoicism which Manilius constantly dwells upon in
his advocacy of a science that will relieve man of his cares and
bring him to godlike wisdom and power by way of a short cut.
Two passages in particular must, in spite of their length, be
quoted in illustration. The first, part of a historical account of the
growth and achievements of science, is taken from near the beginning of the *Astronomica*.

Before that time *Life* was an artless State
Of Reason void, and thoughtless in debate:

Nature lay hid in deepest Night below,
None knew her *wonders*, and none car'd to know:
Upward men lookt, they saw the circling light,
Pleas'd with the Fires, and wondred at the sight:
The *Sun*, when Night came on, withdrawn, they griev'd,
As *dead*, and joy'd next Morn when He reviv'd;
But why the *Nights* grow long or short, the *Day*
Is chang'd, and the *Shades* vary with the Ray,
Shorter at his approach, and longer grown
At his remove, the Causes were unknown:
For *Wit* lay unimprov'd, the desart plains
Were unmanur'd, nor fed the idle Swains:
Ev'n *Gold* dwelt safe in Hills, and none resign'd
Their lives to Seas or wishes to the Wind;
Confin'd their search, they knew themselves alone,
And thought that onely worthy to be known:
But when long time the Wretches thoughts refin'd,
When *Want* had set an edge upon their Mind;
When Men encreast, and Want did boldly press,
And forc'd them to be witty for redress;
Then various Cares their working thoughts employ'd,
And that which *each* invented *all* enjoy'd.
  Then *Corn* first grew, then Fruit enricht the grounds,
And barbarous *noise* was first confin'd to sounds:
Through Seas unknown the *Sailer* then was hurl'd,
And gainfull Traffick joyn'd the distant World:
Then Arts of *War* were found, and Arts of *Peace*,
For Use is always fruitfull in encrease.
New Hints from fettled Arts *Experience* gains,
Instructs our Labour, and rewards our Pains:
Thus into many Streams one Spring divides,
And through the Valleys rouls refreshing Tides.
But these were little things compar'd, they knew
The *Voice* of *Birds*, in Entrails *Fates* could view;
Burst *Snakes* with charms, and in a *Bullock's* bloud,
See *Rage* appeas'd, or fear an *angry* God.
They call'd up *Ghosts*, mov'd deepest Hell, the Sun
Could stop, and force a Night upon his Noon;
Then make him rise at Night, for all submit
To constant *Industry*, and piercing *Wit*.
Nor stopt they here, unwearied Industry
Rose boldly up and mounted through the Sky,

Saw all that could be seen, view'd *Nature*'s Laws,
And *young* Effects still lying in their Cause.
What wings the *Lightning*, why from watry Clouds
The *Thunder* breaks, and roars the wrath of Gods.
What raiseth *Storms*, what makes the *Winds* to blow,
Why *Summer*'s Hail's more stiff than *Winter*'s Snow:
What *fires* Earth's Entrails, what doth *shake* the Ball,
Why *Tempests* rattle, and why *Rain* doth fall:
All this she view'd, and did their *modes* explain,
And taught us to admire no more in vain.
Heaven was disarm'd, mad *Whirlwinds* rul'd above,
And *Clouds* and *Vapors* thundred instead of *Jove*.

    These things explain'd, their hidden Causes known,
The *Mind* grew strong, and ventur'd boldly on;
For rais'd so high, from that convenient rise
She took her flight, and quickly reacht the Skies;
To every *Constellation* Shapes and Names
Assign'd, and markt them out their proper frames;
Then view'd their Course, and saw the *Orbs* were mov'd
As *Heaven* did guide, and as the *World* approv'd;
That *Chance* was baffled whilst their Whirls create
The interchang'd *Variety* of Fate.

                                   [I, 66-112; pp. 5-7]

The second of these extracts is from the concluding section of
Book IV, a hymn to human reason.

    Fond Mortals! why should we our selves abuse?
Nor use those Powers which *God* permits to use?
Basely detract from the Celestial mind,
And close our Eyes, endeavouring to be blind?
We see the Skies, then why should we despair
To know the Fatal Office of each Star?
To open Nature, to unvail her Face,
Go in, and tread the Order of the Maze?
Why should we not employ the Gifts bestow'd
By Heaven, in knowing the kind Author of the Good?
Our Work grows short, we may surround the Ball,
Make the whole World our own, and live in all:
Through what remains, we now with Ease may pierce,
Take, and enjoy the Captive Universe:

Our Parent Nature we, her parts, descry,
And Heaven-born Souls affect their Father Skie:
For who can doubt that *God* resides in Man,
That Souls from Heaven descend, and when the Chain
Of Life is broke, return to Heaven again?
   As in the Greater *World* aspiring Flame,
Earth, Water, Air, make the Material Frame;
But through these Members a Commanding Soul
Infus'd, directs the Motions of the whole;
So 'tis in *Man*, the lesser World, the Case
Is Clay, unactive, and an Earthly Mass;
Bloods Circling Streams the Purple Soul convey,
The Ruling *Mind* uniting to the Clay:
Then who can wonder that the *World* is known
So well by Man, since he himself is One?
The same Composure in his Form is shew'd,
And *Man's* the little Image of the *God*.
   Now other Creatures view, how mean their Birth,
The Rubbish, and the Burdens of the Earth:
Some hang in Air, some float upon the Waves,
Born for our use, and bred to be our Slaves.
All their Enjoyments are confin'd to Sense,
The easie Works of wary Providence.
But since they Reason want, their Tongues are mute,
How mean, how low a Creature is a Brute?
No Mysteries disclos'd, commend their Parts,
Nor are they Subjects capable of Arts;
How hard the Labour, yet how often vain
To bring them foolishly to Ape a Man?
   But ruling Man extends his larger sway
Beyond himself, and makes the World obey;
Wild Beasts are tam'd, The Fields are forc't to bear,
And Recompence the Labours of the Share.
In vain the Sea disjoyns the distant Shores,
His Sails the Winds command, the Floods his Ores.
Alone erect his Form doth nobly rise,
Up to the Stars he lifts his Starry Eyes,
And takes a nearer Prospect of the Skies:
He searches *Jove*, and whilst his Thoughts do trace
He kindred Stars, in them he finds his Race.
No outside Knowledge fills his vast Desires,

The more he riseth, he the more aspires.
. . . .
      Besides, the World is eager to be known,
Our search provoking still; for rouling on
It shews us all its parts, displays its Light,
And constantly intrudes upon our Sight:
His Face unvail'd, *God* doth so plainly shew,
That if we will but look, we needs must know:
He draws our Eyes, nor doth our search forbid;
What Powers he hides not, he would not have hid:
Then who can think it impiously bold
To search what we're encourag'd to behold?
      Nor think thy force too small, too weak thy *Mind*
Because to *Clay* unequally confin'd;
Its Power is wondrous Great; how small a Mass
Of Gold or Gems, exceeds vast Heaps of Brass?
How little is the Apple of the Eye?
And yet at once, he takes in half the Sky:
Nor dreads the disproportion to the Sense,
The Organ small, the Object is immense:
And from the narrow limits of the Heart,
The Active Soul doth vigorous Life impart
To all the Limbs, its Sway the Members own,
Wide is its Empire from its petty Throne.
      Man know thy Powers, and not observe thy Size,
Thy noble Power in piercing *Reason* lies,
And *Reason* conquers all, and rules the Skies.
                        [IV, 866-910, 915-932; pp. 40-42]

In these passages Manilius comes near to achieving a classic expression of an attitude that recurs from age to age, that of a perfervid faith in the capabilities of human science. The first extract contains what are probably Manilius's best-known lines, to which Pope often alludes.

      [ratio] . . . solvitque animis miracula rerum
      eripuitque Iovi fulmen viresque tonandi
      et sonitum ventis concessit, nubibus ignem,
                        [I, 103-105]

("Reason . . . removed the wonder of things from men's minds,

snatched the bolt and the might of the thunder from Jove, and gave the sound to the winds and the fire to the clouds.") Reuben A. Brower has written illuminatingly about the various modes of "marvelling" in the *Essay*, especially in Epistle I, and their different poetic tones;[1] and I have come to believe that in writing as he did, Pope meant to restore the _wonder_ of things to men's minds and to oppose the attitude implied in these lines.[2]

These passages seem to have been thought particularly modern in their relevance, and Creech had emphasized this in some of the material he had supplied, for example the couplet

> And thence they fixt unalterable Laws,
> Settling the *same* Effect on the *same* Cause.

But even before Creech, the modernity of Manilius had been recognized in a way that, perhaps more than any other that could be devised, would connect him with the progress of science. When Newton's *Principia* was published in 1687, Edmond Halley inserted at the beginning a set of verses (given at the end of this chapter) of recognizably Manilian cast, reminiscent of the passages just quoted, as well as others. Evidently he considered that Manilius was the most suitable model for a tribute to a scientist. He claims that Newton had conquered the last secrets of the universe and dispelled the darkness of former ages: mankind should recognize the power of the God-given human mind, which sets men far above the beasts. He compares Newton's discoveries favorably with the framing of laws, the founding of cities, and the invention of bread, wine, and writing, which have only increased our comfort, whereas Newton has made us the guest of the gods. Although no mathematician, Pope must surely at some time have had the curiosity to open the *Principia*, where he would at once have found Halley's poem and recognized the Manilian parody. He would have been reminded of it by the astronomer J. T. Desaguliers's *The Newtonian System of the World, the Best Model of Government* (1728), whose importance among the poems published at the time of Newton's death is emphasized by Marjorie Nicolson.[3] Desaguliers's notes acknowledge Halley's influence on the following lines:

But *Newton* the unparallel'd, whose Name
No Time will wear out in the Book of Fame,
Cælestial Science has promoted more,
Than all the Sages that have shone before.
Nature compell'd, his piercing Mind, obeys,
And gladly shews him all her secret Ways;
'Gainst *Mathematicks* she has no Defence,
And yields t' experimental Consequence:
His tow'ring Genius, from its certain Cause,
Ev'ry Appearance, a *priori* draws,
And shews th' *Almighty Architect*'s unalter'd Laws.

[113-123]

But we can find direct evidence from Pope himself that he looked on Manilius as a suitable text to apply to Newton and the achievements of modern science, in a line of Creech's that we have already seen, "Nature lay hid in deepest Night below" which with the omission of two words and the insertion of "Nature's laws," which occurs on Creech's next page, gives the first line of the epitaph on Newton (1730), "Nature, and Nature's Laws lay hid in Night."

Pope (if we may digress) was not the only poet to use Manilian material when writing of science, as may be seen from William Powell Jones's *The Rhetoric of Science*. Jones identifies various commonplace topics that have parallels in the *Astronomica*; and although there often are, no doubt, other sources, such as the *De Rerum Natura*, echoes of Creech's words occasionally seem to be audible. Such commonplaces are the praise of scientific achievement; the "cosmic voyage" of the great scientist, often Newton, which is more than once described in terms recalling the ascent of "unwearied Industry"; a passage, shortly to be quoted, beginning "Wings raise my feet"; the appeal to the order of the universe to prove its divine origin; and the circulation of water. Two amusing examples of plagiarism instead of borrowing can be given from among Jones's numerous and wide-ranging quotations. An anonymous poem of 1737 called *Order* contains these lines:

Rains feed the earth, nor does the earth deny
To send 'em back in vapours to the sky;
Seas fill the springs, the springs again repay
Their grateful tribute to the flowing sea;
Night follows day, seasons the year divide
'Twixt winter's nakedness and summer's pride.

For the first four lines, see the extract from Book II quoted near the beginning of this chapter. The last line is taken word for word from one of Manilius's philosophical passages (I, 483-531; p. 22). The translation of this passage ends with the couplet

'Tis not from *Chance*; the Motion speaks aloud
The wise and steddy conduct of the *God*,

which appears again in Matthew Tomlinson's *The Trinity*, written in 1726,

'Tis not by chance; these motions speak aloud,
The wise, th' unerring conduct of a God.

Pope cannot be followed in his reversals, contradictions, and other distortions without some attention to verbal niceties. We may suitably take an example from the opening of the *Essay*, where Pope announces his theme by inviting Bolingbroke to

Expatiate free o'er all this scene of Man;
A mighty Maze! but not without a plan;
. . . .
The latent tracts, the giddy heights explore
Of all who blindly creep, or sightless soar,
[I, 5-6, 11-12]

seemingly echoing:

Wings raise my feet, I'm pleas'd to *mount* on high,
Trace all the Mazes of the *liquid* Sky,
Their various turnings, and their whirls declare,
And live in the vast regions of the Air:
I'll know the Stars . . .
I'll search the Depths, the most remote recess.
[I, 14 ff. with added material; p. 2]

Here Pope seems to be deliberately substituting the maze of man for the mazes of the sky as a fit subject for inquiry; however, just as the astrologer will "trace all the mazes," so too has Pope's maze a plan. The word *expatiate* seems to be suggested by the Latin

> iuvat ire per ipsum
> aera, et immenso spatiantem vivere caelo;

and since *spatiari* means "to walk," it seems that it may also have been echoed in the original form of line 6 of the *Essay*, "A mighty maze! of walks without a plan." We may notice also the parallel between the stars and the depths, which Creech makes Manilius say he will know, and Pope's latent tracts and giddy heights; and perhaps there is a suggestion that the astrologer who cries, "Wings raise my feet," is one of those who "sightless soar." Halley is not far from Manilius here, for example, in these lines:

> superum penetrare domos atque ardua caeli
> scandere, sublimis genii concessit acumen.

Pope turns immediately to the attack on "reasoning pride" which forms one of the main themes of the *Essay* and particularly of the first two epistles. He is anxious that man should keep to his true place in the scheme of things and not take too high a view of his own powers. This concern is the opposite of that frequently expressed in the *Astronomica*, where, as we have seen, the poet urges man to use his reason to become like God and upbraids him for his timidity,

> Fond Mortals! why should we our selves abuse?
> Nor use those Powers which *God* permits to use?
> Basely detract from the Celestial mind,
> And close our Eyes, endeavouring to be blind?

Pope seems to imitate this passage while reversing its sense:

> Presumptuous Man! the reason wouldst thou find,
> Why form'd so weak, so little, and so blind!

> [I, 35-36]

Manilius deplores men's "puny fear" and incites them to transgress God's *limites certi*:

> But what avail my Songs, if all refuse
> The profer'd Aid of my obliging Muse?
> If puny fear forbids our Hopes to rise,
> To enter boldly, and enjoy the Skies?

Pope, seemingly with these lines in mind, takes the contrary position,

> In Pride, in reas'ning Pride, our error lies;
> All quit their sphere, and rush into the skies.
> [I, 123-124]

To reduce man's pride, Pope asks ironic questions:

> He, who thro' vast immensity can pierce,
> See worlds on worlds compose one universe,
> Observe how system into system runs,
> What other planets circle other suns,
> What vary'd being peoples ev'ry star,
> May tell why Heav'n has made us as we are.
> But of this frame the bearings, and the ties,
> The strong connections, nice dependencies,
> Gradations just, has thy pervading soul
> Look'd thro'? or can a part contain the whole?
> [I, 23-33]

But when Manilius asks similar questions, they are not ironic.

> Who could know *Heaven*, unless that *Heaven* bestow'd
> The Knowledge? or find *God*, but part of *God*?
> How could the Space immense be e're confin'd
> Within the compass of a narrow Mind?
> How could the Skies, the Dances of the Stars,
> Their Motions adverse, and eternal Wars,
> Unless kind Nature in our Breasts had wrought
> Proportion'd Souls, be subject to our Thought?
> [II, 115-122; p. 54]

After more in the same strain, he starts his detailed revelations by
telling us the sex of each sign of the zodiac. It is amusing to notice
how neatly Pope's "can a part contain the whole?" answers the
first couplet in this extract. In Book III there is a similar passage,

> For who can in his narrow Breast comprise
> The World immense, and who observe the Skies,
> Which with eternal Revolutions move,
> And Circling, measure the vast Orb above?
> What Diligence can e're describe its Face,
> What Art can fix in so immense a space?
>
> [III, 211-215; p. 105]

Again, the questions are not rhetorical; it is the poet himself
whose muse, as he assures us,

> is eager to disclose
> The nicest Secrets; which observ'd, impart
> *Fate*'s Laws, and prove the surest Guides to *Art*.
>
> [III, 43-46; pp. 98-99]

Yet again, when Pope writes,

> When the proud steed shall know why Man restrains
> His fiery course, or drives him o'er the plains;
> When the dull Ox, why now he breaks the clod,
> Is now a victim, and now AEgypt's God:
> Then shall Man's pride and dulness comprehend
> His actions', passions', being's, use and end;
> Why doing, suff'ring, check'd, impell'd; and why
> This hour a slave, the next a deity,
>
> [I, 61-68]   ·

he seems to be making fun of the science that pretends to understand God's purpose and to expound the detailed workings of
fate.

> See *Marius* ride with *Cimbrian* Lawrels Crown'd,
> Then in the Dungeon stretcht upon the ground;
> Now *Slave*, now *Consul*, *Consul*, *Slave* again,

His *Curule* Chair, succeeded by a *Chain*.

. . . .

These wondrous changes *Fate* and *Stars* advance.

[IV, 45-49; pp. 5-6]

In such passages Pope directly asserts that the power of reason is limited, contradicting the Stoic position. In others he attacks the associated fallacy that man is so greatly superior to the animals that they cannot be considered, by comparison, to have any importance at all in the created scheme. This view is expressed vigorously in these lines from the conclusion of Book IV, as we have already seen.

> Now other Creatures view, how mean their Birth,
> The Rubbish, and the Burdens of the Earth:
> Some hang in Air, some float upon the Waves,
> Born for our Use, and bred to be our Slaves.
> All their Enjoyments are confin'd to Sense,
> The easie Works of wary Providence.
> But since they Reason want, their Tongues are mute,
> How mean, how low a Creature is a Brute?
> No Mysteries disclos'd, commend their Parts,
> Nor are they Subjects capable of Arts;
> How hard the Labour, yet how often vain
> To bring them foolishly to Ape a Man?

Here Creech has been driven, or has seized the chance offered, by defective manuscripts to supply much material from other sources, some of it at least being doctrine common to both Epicureans and Stoics. Halley too links the superiority of man to his ability to make scientific discoveries, or "disclose mysteries," in words that are more moderate in substance and far more tactful in expression,

> caeligenae vires dinoscite mentis,
> a pecudum vita longe lateque remotae.

Pope, the great animal lover who believed dogs to be little below humans in the chain of being, had to reject this philosophy absolutely, and his rejection seems to be reflected in more than

one passage of the *Essay*. Take for example the scornful rebuke of pride in Epistle III. The third line quoted may also echo the claim in the *Astronomica* (III, 73; p. 99) that man is the "chiefest object of Nature's cares."

> Has God, thou fool! work'd solely for thy good,
> Thy job, thy pastime, thy attire, thy food?
> . . . .
> Know, Nature's children all divide her care;
> The fur that warms a monarch, warm'd a bear.
> While Man exclaims, "See all things for my use!"
> "See man for mine!" replies a pamper'd goose;
> And just as short of Reason he must fall,
> Who thinks all made for one, not one for all.
>
> [III, 27-28, 43-48]

The questioning of Stoic reasonableness is the unkindest cut. Another passage makes clear Pope's fundamental objection, which is that to leave too great an interval between man and the rest of creation would destroy the coherence of the universe.

> See, thro' this air, this ocean, and this earth,
> All matter quick, and bursting into birth.
> Above, how high progressive life may go!
> Around, how wide! how deep extend below!
> Vast chain of being,
>
> [I, 233-237]

and so on. The verbal imitation (note "view" and "see," the mention of earth, air, and water, and the rhyme of the opening couplet) of Creech's lines beginning "Now other Creatures view" points up the contrast with the impious claims of reasoning pride.

Yet another echo of Creech's lines seems to underlie the rebuke offered to science in Epistle II, "Go, wond'rous creature! mount where Science guides" (II, 19) recalling Halley's *surgite mortales*, and the later lines on Newton,

> Superior beings, when of late they saw
> A mortal Man unfold all Nature's law,

> Admir'd such wisdom in an earthly shape,
> And shew'd a NEWTON as we shew an Ape.
>
> [II, 31-34]

These may be compared with

> No Mysteries disclos'd, commend their Parts,
> Nor are they Subjects capable of Arts;
> How hard the Labour, yet how often vain
> To bring them foolishly to Ape a Man?

Creech (for there is no basis for these lines in the Latin) is emphasizing the distance between men and the beasts who lack human reason, whereas Pope is emphasizing the distance between the angels and even the man who above all others had the power of reason and who disclosed the greatest mysteries. An animal cannot ape a man, and Newton to an angel is as but an ape is to us. Pope's lines that shortly follow,

> Trace Science then, with Modesty thy guide;
> First strip off all her equipage of Pride,
> . . . .
> Then see how little the remaining sum,
> Which serv'd the past, and must the times to come,
>
> [II, 43-44; 51-52]

throw doubt on the value of scientific progress and embody another of Pope's complaints against reasoning pride, which lacks respect not only for the rest of creation but for man's own past and his greatest achievements. Such an attitude is implied several times in the *Astronomica*, for example at the very beginning,

> At what the *Ancients* with a wild amaze
> And ignorant wonder were content to gaze,
> My Verse brings down from Heav'n, design'd to show
> Celestial secrets to the World below;
>
> [I, 3 with added material; p. 2]

or again in the long passage we have seen,

> Before that time *Life* was an artless state,
> Of Reason void, and thoughtless in debate.

Halley has something of the same thought:

> quae toties animos veterum torsere Sophorum,
> quaeque Scholas frustra rauco certamine vexant,
> obvia conspicimus, nubem pellente Mathesi;

and he goes on to place the achievements of scientists far above those of the founders of cities and the discoverers of arts and crafts, which are merely useful, whereas Newton has made us the guests of the gods. Such claims as these probably contributed their stimulus to Pope's rebuke to science and his recognition of the achievements of the past,

> Nor think, in NATURE'S STATE they blindly trod;
> The state of Nature was the reign of God,
>   [III, 147-148]

and his praise for the founding of cities and for the discovery of arts and law.

Again, reasoning pride distorts man's own nature by paying regard only to the intellect, as in the following passage from the introduction to Book III:

> Then come, who e're thou art that bring'st a Mind
> To know high Truth, and patient Thoughts to find;
> Hear solid Reason, and go on to gain
> True serious Knowledge, but neglect the vain;
> No Kings at *Aulis* sworn, no tales of *Troy*
> With *Priam's* tears, or *Helen's* fatal Joy,
> Nor hope sweet Verse, and curious turns to find,
> I'll leave thy Passions, and instruct thy Mind.
>   [III, 36-39 with added material; p. 98]

There are interesting anticipations here of later forms of Philistinism, a rejection of the highest achievements of art represented by the Homeric stories in favor of "true solid knowledge," and the

assumption that the passions are separate from the mind. This last assertion distorts, and fails to perceive, the true nature of man, who comprises reason and passion; and the man who thinks he has freed his mind of the *miracula rerum* will go dangerously wrong,

> Alas what wonder! Man's superior part
> Uncheck'd may rise, and climb from art to art:
> But when his own great work is but begun,
> What Reason weaves, by Passion is undone;
>
> [II, 39-43]

and this is true even of the man who has charted the comets and is therefore praised by Halley. The underlying fault of reasoning pride is thus to be seen as a failure of self-knowledge combined with a claim to know everything else, including even God (*inquiritque Iovem*, or "he searches God"): indeed, self-knowledge is dismissed as unimportant,

> Confin'd their search, they knew themselves alone,
> And thought that onely worthy to be known;

whereas the final message of Pope in the *Essay* is that self-knowledge is all-important: "Know then thyself, presume not God to scan" (II, 1) and "And all our Knowledge is, OURSELVES TO KNOW" (IV, 398).

Pope makes it very plain that he convicts science of pride, but we should not overlook his attack on its dullness, which consists of the attempt to discover things that are better hidden. Here again the *Astronomica* seems to provide an example, which Pope employs in Epistle I, "Heav'n from all creatures hides the book of Fate" (I, 77). It seems clear from lines that follow, and particularly from those about the lamb, that the knowledge which most of all would make a happy life impossible is that of the day of our death. The *Astronomica* incessantly promises to unfold Fate ("I'll turn *Fate*'s books," writes Creech in the opening passage); and there is a topic of astrology devoted to the calculation of the length of life.

[The muse] next must show
What length of Times the several Signs bestow:
This must be known when in your search for Fate
You measure Life, and fix the gloomy Date.
[III, 562-566; p. 119]

The calculations are given without any hint that the knowledge
they yield might be unwelcome; one may quote the lines on the
influence of the sixth "station" (a division of the sky), which

but *Twelve* [years] bestows, then Death destroys
The Parents Hopes, and crops the growing Boys;
Diseases following, from their Birth create
A feeble Frame, and fit the Prey for Fate.
[III, 617-618; p. 121]

Pope at twelve years old, attacked by a serious disease, would have
fully grasped the folly of being wise about such things. (Compare
the preceding lines with Epistle II, lines 133 to 136.)

This section may fittingly end with a brief look at the lines
on the poor Indian, which have often (but not, of course, in the
Twickenham edition) been seen as an ornamental passage or
"beauty of Pope," only loosely connected with their context.
However, in the light of what we have learned, they will reveal a
further meaning.

Lo! the poor Indian, whose untutor'd mind
Sees God in clouds, or hears him in the wind.
[I, 99-100]

In this couplet, surely Pope is alluding to, and neatly refuting, the
boast that reason

solvitque animis miracula rerum
eripuitque Iovi fulmen viresque tonandi
et sonitum ventis concessit, nubibus ignem;
[I, 103-105]

which we should read with the translation of the immediately
following lines,

> These things explain'd, their hidden Causes known,
> The *Mind* grew strong, and ventur'd boldly on;
> For rais'd so high, from that convenient rise
> She took her flight, and quickly reacht the Skies.

The scientist thinks he has "explained" part of nature by attributing thunder and lightning to the wind and the clouds; but the Indian perceives the wonder of the wind and the clouds themselves, and though his mind is untutored (not "strong"), he knows that the scientist has explained nothing. It is a warning to us not to "Snatch from his hand [*eripere*] the balance and the rod" (I, 121).

> His soul proud Science never taught to stray
> Far as the solar walk, or milky way.
>
> [I, 101-102]

Pope has a manuscript note naming Cicero and Manilius as sources for the ancient belief that the souls of the just went to the Milky Way. The Indian is not so ambitious; he does not claim to inherit the sky or to "Take, and enjoy the Captive Universe."

> Yet simple Nature to his hope has giv'n,
> Behind the cloud-topt hill, an humbler heav'n;
> Some safer world in depth of woods embrac'd,
> Some happier island in the watry waste,
> Where slaves once more their native land behold,
> No fiends torment, no Christians thirst for gold!
>
> [I, 103-108]

The Indian's idea of heaven projects his inner harmony with nature, his ability to live with the elements, and his desire to shun strife.

> To Be, contents his natural desire,
> He asks no Angel's wing, no Seraph's fire.
>
> [I, 109-110]

This couplet seems to be adapted from Creech's

> No outside Knowledge fills his vast Desires,
> The more he riseth, he the more aspires.

Unlike the devotee of proud science, the Indian has decided to
live, not know; his desire is natural, not vast; he does not wish to
cross the *limes certus*, or "insuperable line," which divides man
from the angels, by rising first on wings, through the air, to the
empyrean.

> But thinks, admitted to that equal sky,
> His faithful dog shall bear him company.
>
> [I, 111-112]

Other creatures are not to him "the rubbish of the earth" or slaves,
but friends not far below us on the great scale,[4] and the sky is their
cognatum caelum also. The lines on the poor Indian, in fact, re-
semble the story of Lodona in *Windsor Forest* and the game of
ombre in the *Rape of the Lock* in that they epitomize the poem in
which they are found.

III

In Epistle IV Pope moves on to discuss happiness, whose nature and value have much puzzled mankind. The opening of the
epistle follows much the same pattern as others of his poems on
difficult subjects, for example, the *Essay on Criticism*, which
deals with the contentious matter of literary values. There seems
to be a resemblance to the opening of the *Metamorphoses*, where
we see first the Chaos that lay before the *opifex rerum*, then his
way of resolving it into order by the separation and arrangement
of the jarring parts. In the *Essay on Criticism* we see first a scene of
bewilderment, confusion, and false values, then we are given the
solution, "follow Nature." Here also in Epistle IV the opening
depicts the chaotic speculations of the sages, behind which we
seem to hear *frigida pugnabant calidis*,

> Ask of the Learn'd the way, the Learn'd are blind,
> This bids to serve, and that to shun mankind;
> Some place the bliss in action, some in ease,
> Those call it Pleasure, and Contentment these,
>
> [IV, 19-22]

and so on. Then comes the resolution, "Take Nature's path"; and it seems that this again means that we are to see the *summum bonum* of happiness as an expression of *concordia discors*, a state in which the balance of the whole will comprehend any local deficiencies:

> Obvious her goods, in no extreme they dwell,
> There needs but thinking right, and meaning well;
> And mourn our various portions as we please,
> Equal is Common Sense, and Common Ease.
>
> [IV, 31-34]

However, we should also, as I believe, look to the *Astronomica*, since we shall find in the Stoic doctrine of fate some account of human destiny, our various portions, in their cosmological setting. Creech's words are worth repeating:

> This Infinite Mind hath made one general decree concerning the Government of the lower World, and executes it by giving such and such powers to the Celestial Bodies, as are sufficient and proper to produce the design'd Effects: This *Decree* thus executed they call *Fate*, and upon this Principle their whole System of *Astrology* depends.

The doctrine is connected with that of Creation and *concordia discors* in the following passage:

> When Nature order'd this vast Frame to rise
> . . . .
> . . . [she] made *Earth*, Water, Air,
> And *Fire*, each other mutually repair;
> That Concord might these differing parts controul,
> And Leagues of mutual Aid support the whole;
> That nothing which the *Skies* embrace might be
> From Heaven's supreme Command and Guidance free,
> On *Man* the chiefest Object of her Cares
> Long time she thought, then hung his Fates on Stars
> . . . .
> . . . [which] sometimes ruling, sometimes rul'd, create

The strange and various intercourse of Fate.

. . . .

      they have not equal Shares
Of common Power, each *Fortune* claims its Stars.
Our Studies, Poverty, Wealth, Joy and Grief

. . . .

She parcels out.

                          [III, 47-48, 52-58, 76-80; p. 99]

Of course, the idea of a general cosmic order and balance, embracing (and reflected in) the pattern of human fortunes, need not entail any executive power for the stars or the acceptance of astrology and the ability of man to read fate. Fate and the lots of mankind are discussed again at the opening of Book IV, an eloquent passage well translated by Creech (where, incidentally, Manilius comes nearest to expounding the Stoic ethic of endurance):

> Why should our Time run out in useless years,
> Of anxious Troubles and tormenting Fears?
> Why should deluding Hopes disturb our ease,
> Vain to pursue, yet eager to possess?
> With no Success, and no Advantage crown'd,
> Why should we still tread on th' *unfinisht* Round?
> Grown gray in Cares, pursue the senseless strife,
> And seeking how to Live, consume a Life?
> The more we have, the meaner is our Store;
> The unenjoying craving *Wretch* is Poor:
> But *Heaven* is kind, with bounteous Hand it grants
> A fit supply for Nature's sober wants:
> She asks not much, yet Men press blindly on,
> And heap up more, to be the more undone:
> By *Luxury*, they *Rapine*'s Force maintain,
> What that scrapes up, flows out in *Luxury* again;
> And to be squander'd, or to raise debate,
> Is the great only use of an Estate.
>   Vain Man forbear, of Cares, unload thy Mind,
> Forget thy Hopes, and give thy Fears to Wind;
> For *Fate* rules all, its stubborn Laws must sway
> The lower World, and *Man* confin'd obey.

As we are Born we Dye, our Lots are cast,
And our first Hour disposeth of our last.
Then as the influence of the Stars ordains,
To Empires *Kings* are doom'd, and *Slaves* to Chains.
Then Poverty, that common Fate comes down,
(Few Stars are Regal, and design a Crown)
What make a *Wit*, a *Knave*, a *Saint*, or *Dunce*,
Are hudled then together, and fixt at once.
The Ills that are *ordain'd* we must endure,
From not *Decreed* how fatally secure?
Prayers are too weak to check fixt Destinies,
And Vows too slow to catch the Fate that flies.
Whether with Glory rais'd, or clogg'd with Scorn,
The State, that then is *setled*, must be born.

[IV, 1-22; pp. 3-4]

This passage is illustrated in Creech's frontispiece. On a banner in the sky can be seen part of the line *"nascentes morimur, finisque ab origine pendet,"* which Creech translates by the couplet printed in italics. It is an important line, referring not to the fleetingness of life, as might be thought, but to the persistence of the natal character throughout life; Pope imitates it several times. A series of arguments follows this introductory passage, designed to show against the Epicureans that fate, not chance, rules the world. The perhaps not very convincing logic behind most of the arguments is that some effects are so strange that mere chance could not have produced them, and they must be the work of the stronger power of fate. One of the arguments is of interest to us:

To fewer Days they do not cramp the *Poor*,
Nor brib'd by Wealth, enlarge the *Rich* with more;
There Riches lose their force, the shining Years
Of glorious *Tyrants* must be turn'd in Tears;
They dig a Grave for *Kings*, and fix the Day;
How great must be that Power which Crowns obey!
  Successless *Vertue* sinks whilst *Vice* prevails,
And *Folly* wins the Prize when *Prudence* fails:
He argues ill that from the *Fortune* draws
The goodness or the badness of a Cause:
Successes *Merit* do not always Crown,

> Midst good and bad Men they are blindly thrown,
> Without *Respect*, fixt fatally on *One*.
>
> [IV, 89-97; p. 8]

We should also look at the last of Manilius's arguments, where, as Creech puts it, he "endeavours to take off some Objections that might be rationally propos'd against this Doctrin;" the logic of this passage is rather obscure in the translation.

> To this there's one Objection; *Fate* denies
> Rewards to *Vertue*, and must plead for Vice:
> Absurd; for who less hates a *Poysonous* Weed
> Because 'tis bred from *Necessary* Seed?
> Or who loves *Corn* the less; who hates the *Vine*
> Because by *Nature* rais'd, and not *Design*?
> Thus Virtuous Minds deserve the greater Love,
> Since *Heaven* consents, and all the *Stars* approve;
> And we should hate those more whom *Fates* have sent
> To commit Crimes and suffer Punishment;
> For how, or whence these noxious faults begin
> No matter, since each is certainly a Sin.
>
> [IV, 108-117; p. 9]

Within this cosmic scheme, Pope accepts and moralizes the doctrine of the lots. Manilius's concern is to win students of astrology, and to him fate is something that can be explained by science but cannot be questioned and has no ethical meaning; when he says, at the end of the second passage just quoted, "sors est sua cuique ferenda," he is stating a fact, not a duty. Pope does not dispute the doctrine, as far as it goes. In the *Temple of Fame* he had already written how

> fickle *Fortune* reigns,
> And undiscerning, scatters Crowns and Chains,[5]
>
> [296-297]

and again in Epistle IV he writes,

> Fortune in Men has some small diff'rence made,
> One flaunts in rags, one flutters in brocade,

> The cobler apron'd, and the parson gown'd,
> The friar hooded, and the monarch crown'd,
>
> [IV, 195-198]

lines that seem to be inspired by Creech's frontispiece, where we see all these figures and, in the foreground, both flaunting and fluttering. However, Pope is attempting to vindicate the ways of God and must attack the problem, or what some think is the problem, of suffering and the injustice, or seeming injustice, of Providence. It is not my business here to try to judge the success of his arguments but merely to seek to establish their connection with the *Astronomica*. We have already seen how "mutual wants" form a *concordia discors* that increases the sum of happiness; Pope goes on to contend that hope and fear keep the balance by tempering the unhappiness of the unfortunate and the joy of the lucky:

> Fortune her gifts may variously dispose,
> And these be happy call'd, unhappy those;
> But Heav'n's just balance equal will appear,
> While those are plac'd in Hope, and these in Fear:
> Not present good or ill, the joy or curse,
> But future views of better, or of worse.
>
> [IV, 67-72]

Here Pope finds a use for emotions that we are urged in the *Astronomica* to abandon,

> Vain Man forbear, of Cares, unload thy Mind,
> Forget thy Hopes, and give thy Fears to Wind.

and which are so deeply embedded in human nature that it is foolish to think we could ever be without them. Besides, hope, at least, has been given to man as a blessing (see Epistle I, line 94).

Pope seems to have derived other arguments from the couplet

> He argues ill that from the *Fortune* draws
> The goodness or the badness of a cause.

He concedes that "The good or bad the gifts of Fortune gain" (IV, 83), but it is not enough merely to gain them, they must also be enjoyed, for mere good fortune is not happiness, and this the bad cannot do to the full, "But these less taste them, as they worse obtain" (IV, 84). Thus the Stoic doctrine is true, but inadequate, since it leaves out the most important term in the equation, the moral state of happiness. Pope goes on to reinforce the point,

> Oh blind to truth, and God's whole scheme below,
> Who fancy Bliss to Vice, to Virtue Woe!
>
> [IV, 93-94]

The first line of this couplet seems to take up and intensify Creech's mild phrase "he argues ill;" though good or bad fortune is not necessarily a guide to the virtue or vice of the possessor, it is a worse mistake to think that this is a sign of the unjust distribution of the true rewards. Pope develops this argument at length.

Pope gives another answer to the difficulty when he denies that virtue should even expect good fortune or any kind of reward except that which it creates for itself:

> "But sometimes Virtue starves, while Vice is fed."
> What then? Is the reward of Virtue bread?
> . . . .
>   What nothing earthly gives, or can destroy,
> The soul's calm sun-shine, and the heart-felt joy,
> Is Virtue's prize.
>
> [IV, 149-150, 167-169]

The first line quoted here is a translation of Book IV, line 94, "*quin etiam infelix virtus et noxia felix*," for which Creech gives, as we have seen, "Successless *Vertue* sinks whilst *Vice* prevails;" here Pope follows the contention

> He argues ill that from the *Fortune* draws
> The goodness or the badness of a Cause.

The latter lines seem to draw on our fourth extract from the *Astronomica*,

> Thus Virtuous Minds deserve the greater Love,
> Since *Heaven* consents, and all the Stars approve,

as the strong verbal resemblances suggest ("virtue's prize" is what "virtuous minds deserve;" "nothing earthly" is "heaven, and all the stars;" and "the soul's calm sunshine" replaces, with no very great distortion of sense, "the greater love").

We return to the passage that we have quoted earlier in this very brief examination of the epistle:

> Honour and shame from no Condition rise;
> Act well your part, there all the honour lies.
> Fortune in Men has some small diff'rence made,
> One flaunts in rags, one flutters in brocade,
> The cobler apron'd, and the parson gown'd,
> The friar hooded, and the monarch crown'd.
> "What differ more (you cry) than crown and cowl?"
> I'll tell you, friend, A Wise man and a Fool.[6]
>
> > [IV, 193-200]

Here, in the first couplet, we find *sors est sua cuique ferenda* used in a moral sense, "act *well* your part," which is, as Mack points out, the central doctrine of traditional ethics and is one of the moral climaxes of the epistle. The gifts of fortune are nothing to the worth that makes the man.

IV

So much for doctrine, but before concluding, I should observe that the influence of the *Astronomica* on the *Essay* is also to be seen in particulars that are incidental to the doctrine — in ornamental and illustrative passages, and even, perhaps, in style and tone. A small selection of borrowings may be of interest. One shows how Pope's knowledge of gardening enabled him to improve a metaphor, and from this —

> How different Vertues Reign, how different Crimes?
> Mens Manners are as various as the Climes.

> Like Trees transplanted by the Farmer's Toyl;
> Vice turns to Vertue, in another Soyl,
>
> [IV, 732-733, p. 34]

produce this —

> As fruits ungrateful to the planter's care
> On savage stocks inserted learn to bear;
> The surest Virtues thus from Passions shoot,
> Wild Nature's vigor working at the root.
>
> [II, 181-184]

The typical translation of "farmer's toil" into "planter's care" is proof that the resemblance is not accidental. The next example shows the genesis of a great passage. In Book IV of the *Astronomica* we find these lines on the Sagittarius births:

> Bold *Sagittarius*, when he first appears,
> Heats the gay *Birth*, and makes him fam'd for Wars;
> In Triumphs great, the Wonder of the Crowd,
> By Captives carry'd, he almost a God
> Shall climb the *Capitol*, bright fame pursue,
> *Old* Cities raze, or grace the Earth with *New*:
> But ill success, (his Forehead's wreath'd with Frowns)
> Shall wast his Fame, and blast his gather'd Crowns.
> Thus Conquering *Hannibal*, by this Sign betray'd
> Before his flight perceiv'd his Wreaths to fade,
> He paid for *Trebia*'s and for *Cannae*'s fame,
> And recompenc'd our Losses by his shame.
>
> [IV, 560-561; p. 27]

Here surely is to be found the germ of the satire on Marlborough in Epistle IV.

> In hearts of Kings, or arms of Queens who lay,
> How happy! those to ruin, these betray,
> Mark by what wretched steps their glory grows,
> From dirt and sea-weed as proud Venice rose;
> In each how guilt and greatness equal ran,
> And all that rais'd the Hero, sunk the Man.
> Now Europe's laurels on their brows behold,

But stain'd with blood, or ill exchang'd for gold,
Then see them broke with toils, or sunk in ease,
Or infamous for plunder'd provinces.
Oh wealth ill-fated! which no act of fame
E'er taught to shine, or sanctify'd from shame!
What greater bliss attends their close of life?
Some greedy minion, or imperious wife,
The trophy'd arches, story'd halls invade,
And haunt their slumbers in the pompous shade.
Alas! not dazzled with their noon-tide ray,
Compute the morn and ev'ning to the day;
The whole amount of that enormous fame,
A Tale, that blends their glory with their shame!
[IV, 289-308]

Again, some telltale verbal resemblances remain, as in the concluding rhymes of each extract or in the following couplets:

But ill success, (his Forehead's wreath'd with Frowns)
Shall wast his Fame, and blast his gather'd Crowns,

and

Now Europe's laurels on their brows behold,
But stain'd with blood, or ill exchang'd for gold.

An example of a different sort, which shows Pope's diligence in collecting his material, is given by the picture in Epistle III of the ancient patriarch who is master of the four elements,

He from the wond'ring furrow call'd the food,
Taught to command the fire, controul the flood,
Draw forth the monsters of th'abyss profound,
Or fetch th'aerial eagle to the ground.
[III, 219-222]

These arts all seem to reflect the gifts conferred by various constellations. First, Spica, the ear of corn,

The Fields may fear, for those that shall be born
Shall Plough the Ground, and be intent on Corn:

They'll trust their Seed to Clods, whose large Produce
Shall yield the *Sum*, and give increase by *Use*.

[V, 272-275; p. 66]

Notice that Creech has imputed a state of mind, fear, to the fields;
Pope makes the furrows "wonder." The births of Capricorn
command the fire,

But Sacred *Vesta* guards thy fatal Fire,
And thence 'tis guess'd, what Minds thy Rays inspire,
Contracted *Goat*; by thee that Art's infus'd,
Which *Fire* assists,

[IV, 243-246; p. 14]

and so on, for several lines. Aquarius, the next constellation, gives
examples of those who control the flood,

Aquarius pouring out his Urn, imparts
An useful Knowledge in resembling Arts,
To find out Springs, and with new Streams supply
The Barren Countries,

[IV, 259-261; p. 15]

and so on again. "Draw forth the monsters of th'abyss profound"
is the activity of those born under Iugulae, Manilius tells us,

sunt quibus in ponto studium est cepisse ferarum
diversas facies et caeco mersa *profundo*
sternere litoreis *monstrorum* corpora harenis.

[V, 189-191]

Creech has

Another puts to Sea, infests the Lakes,
Draws monstrous Fish, and starts at what he Takes,

[p. 62]

which is further than Pope from the Latin. Finally "Or fetch
th'aerial eagle to the ground" is a fairly close translation of a line
written about those born under Sagitta, the Arrow: "*penden-*

temque suo volucrem deprendere caelo" (V, 296). Creech again is less close.

More examples might be given, but perhaps enough has been said to show that two poets whose own works will probably always remain in the shadows still have a sort of life in the immortal *Essay*.

Halley's Verses in Praise of Newton

This poem was printed in the first edition of the *Principia* and in the subsequent Latin editions. In the first English edition only a few lines of it appeared. I have been unable to find an English translation and so have made my own. Though I may have mistaken Halley's meaning at some points, the general effect is clear. Although this sort of praise of a great sage is a commonplace of ancient poetry, nevertheless it seems possible to detect a special Manilian influence, particularly of the better-known parts of Books I and IV of the *Astronomica*. Compare, for example, Halley's line, "surgite, mortales, terrenas mittite curas" (27) with "solvite, mortales, animos, curasque levate" (IV, 12).

IN VIRI PRAESTANTISSIMI
ISAACI NEWTONI

OPUS HOCCE MATHEMATICO-PHYSICUM
SECULI GENTISQUE NOSTRAE DECUS EGREGIUM

1687

En tibi norma poli, et divae libramina molis,
Computus en Jovis; et quas, dum primordia rerum
Pangeret, omniparens leges violare Creator
Noluit, atque operum quae fundamenta locarit.
   Intima panduntur victi penetralia caeli,
Nec latet extremos quae vis circumrotat orbes.
Sol solio residens ad se jubet omnia prono
Tendere descensu, nec recto tramite currus

Sidereos patitur vastum per inane moveri;
Sed rapit immotis, se centro, singula gyris.
   Jam patet, horrificis quae sit via flexa cometis;
Jam non miramur barbati phaenomena astri.
Discimus hinc tandem qua causa argentea Phoebe
Passibus haud aequis graditur; cur subdita nulli
Hactenus Astronomo numerorum fraena recuset;
Cur remeant Nodi, curque Auges progrediuntur.
Discimus et quantis refluum vaga Cynthia pontum
Viribus impellit, fessis dum fluctibus ulvam
Deserit, ac nautis suspectas nudat arenas;
Alternis vicibus suprema ad litora pulsans.
   Quae toties animos veterum torsere sophorum,
Quaeque scholas frustra rauco certamine vexant,
Obvia conspicimus, nubem pellente Mathesi.
Jam dubios nulla caligine praegravat error,
Queis superum penetrare domos, atque ardua caeli
Scandere, sublimis genii concessit acumen.
   Surgite mortales, terrenas mittite curas:
Atque hinc caeligenae vires dignoscite mentis,
A pecudum vita longe lateque remotae.
   Qui scriptis jussit tabulis compescere caedes,
Furta et adulteria, et perjurae crimina fraudis;
Quive vagis populis circundare moenibus urbes
Auctor erat; Cererisve beavit munere gentes;
Vel qui curarum lenimen pressit ab uva;
Vel qui Niliaca mostravit arundine pictos
Consociare sonos, oculisque exponere voces;
Humanam sortem minus extulit: utpote pauca
Respiciens miserae tantum solamina vitae.
Jam vero superis convivae admittimur, alti
Jura poli tractare licet, jamque abdita caecae
Claustra patent terrae, rerumque immobilis ordo,
Et quae praeteriti latuerunt secula mundi.
   Talia monstrantem mecum celebrate camenis,
Vos o caelicolum gaudentes nectare vesci,
Newtonum clausi reserantem scrinia veri,
Newtonum Musis carum, cui pectore puro
Phoebus adest, totoque incessit numine mentem:
Nec fas est propius mortali attingere divos.

                                   [1-48]

FOR THE PEERLESS
ISAAC NEWTON'S

MATHEMATICO-PHYSICAL WORK, THE CHIEF
GLORY OF OUR AGE AND RACE
1687

Here are the rules of the sky, which balance the divine mass, and here are God's calculations. Here are the laws that the Creator and father of all would not break when he established the beginnings of the universe, and the foundations that he placed for his work.

The heavens have been conquered and their innermost recesses opened, and the force that turns the farthest orbs is hidden no longer. The sun enthroned commands all things to approach him in downward motion. He forbids the chariots of the planets to keep a straight course through the mighty void but whirls each round in a never-changing circle, himself the center.

Now the curved path of the fearsome comets is known, and we marvel no longer at the appearances of a bearded star. From this book we learn at last why silver Phoebe steps with unequal paces; why, unsubdued until now by any astronomer, she has refused to be fettered by mathematics; why her nodes move backwards, her apsides [*aux* — an Arabic word meaning *apsis*] forwards. We learn with how much force wandering Cynthia drives the sea in ebb, when with tired waves it abandons its weeds and uncovers the sands that sailors dread, then in turn beating the top of the shore.

All that so often tormented the sages of old and that troubles the academies with vain and harsh disputes, we now see clearly, as Science dispels the clouds. Now no error oppresses men with darkness and doubt; the intellect of the sublime Genius lets them enter the abodes of the gods and climb the heights of heaven.

Mortals arise, throw off the cares of earth, and learn here the

powers of the heaven-born mind, so far, so widely removed from the state of the beasts!

The men who commanded the crimes of murder, theft, adultery, and perjured fraud to be suppressed by written laws, or first built walled cities for wandering peoples, or blessed mankind with corn, or squeezed the grape to lighten cares, or taught to join painted sounds on the Nile reed and make speech visible, raised the human state by less, for they sought only a few comforts for our wretched life. Now indeed we are admitted as guests by the gods, now we may discourse of the laws of high heaven, now the hidden deeps of the earth are revealed, the eternal order of nature, and all that escaped the earlier ages of mankind.

Praise with me in your songs him who shows us these, poets who joy to feed on celestial nectar: NEWTON who opens the scrolls of hidden truth, NEWTON whom the Muses love, whom in purity of soul Apollo inspires, and whose mind he has entered in all his divinity: a mortal may come no nearer the gods.

CHAPTER 5

The Cosmic Science of Character — the "Epistle to Cobham"

Preliminary Note on the Text:

In the last months of Pope's life, Warburton persuaded him to transpose several passages of the "Epistle to Cobham," which was always so reprinted until the original order was restored in the Twickenham edition. My thesis requires me to follow the original order, and hence all my references are to the Twickenham text. The following comparative table of line numbers shows the transpositions:

Twickenham text	Traditional text
1–22	1–22
23–28	31–36
29–30	23–24
31–34	37–40
35–40	25–30
41–50	41–50
51–109	99–157
110–157	51–98
158–227	158–227
228–247	232–251
248–251	228–231
252–265	252–265

The "Epistle to Cobham," Epistle I of the *Moral Essays*, deals with the problem of reading human nature. The difficulties are

first set out: the variety of types, the imperfections of our own faculties of observation and the distortions they produce, the short time we have to observe, the deceptiveness of appearances, and the impenetrability and inconsistency of character. The key is to find each man's ruling passion, which, once known, will explain everything that seems strange or incomprehensible. There are over fifty examples to illustrate the theory of the poem.

Pope had previously presented character in terms of *concordia discors*, as in

> But ALL subsists by elemental strife;
> And Passions are the elements of Life,
> [*Essay on Man*, I, 169-170]

and in

> This light and darkness in our chaos join'd,
> What shall divide? The God within the mind,
> [Ibid , II, 203-204]

which recalls Sandys's version of the ordering of Chaos: "What God soever this division wrought." As Mack puts it in his introduction to the *Essay on Man*, Pope thinks of character "as a creative achievement, an artistic result, something built out of chaos as God built the world." In this, of course, he is following the cosmological tradition that stretched back through the Renaissance to antiquity. In "To Cobham," perhaps his most elaborate account of character, we might expect to find the same tradition, and indeed cosmology seems to be introduced by the discussion of psychological method with which the poem opens — should our study of human nature be based on books and theory or on the observation of life? Cobham, that clever man of the world, as F. W. Bateson called him, had compared the book-student to a parrot or another talking bird; that is, paradoxically he was not a true philosopher but (like an Epicurean) could only be "right by chance." Pope reminds him that this is an extreme view and that at the other extreme observations also rely on chance, being "drawn

from Guess." There seem to be allusions here to the Epicurean theory of Creation.

In the early part of the poem Pope seems to be presenting human nature as a kind of chaos of contradiction and illusion, and we find a number of terms and concepts which elsewhere are often cosmological: variety, and the strife of our nature and faculties (20–21); the troubled heap of our thoughts (45); the difficulty of balancing our judgment (74). The seeming mutability of man is contrasted with God and Nature, which "only are the same." The key to man is the ruling passion, which in the words of the Argument, "reconciles the seeming or real inconsistency of all his actions" and lies "in what you cannot change." The language here seems to recall at once the reconciliation of the strife of Chaos and Manilius's view of the world (the italics are mine).

> All Mortal Things must change. The fruitfull Plain,
> As Seasons turn, scarce knows her self again.
> . . . .
> Yet safe the World, and *free from Change* doth last.
> . . . .
> [It] still will be, because *'twas still the same.*
>> [I, 515-516, 518, 521; p. 22]

Pope's suggestion seems to be that the microcosm, man, is similar to the macrocosm; beneath the temporary appearances there lies an immutable cosmic reality. Even the chaotic nature of the "flagitious" Wharton (Stephanus defines *akosmia* in the moral sense as *vita flagitiosa*) can be understood by this principle. In the triumphant couplet

> Nature well known, no miracles remain,
> Comets are regular, and Wharton plain,
>> [208-209]

("miracles" was the original reading, replaced by "prodigies" in 1744 at Warburton's instance), we hear echoes of how reason *cepit profundam naturam rerum* and *solvit animis miracula rerum*, words familiar to us and part of the passage that provided Pope

with the first line of Newton's epitaph; and, with this, there is an allusion to Newton's studies of the motion of comets, which Halley had celebrated. Pope's moral discovery, it is implied, is akin to and equal to the physical discoveries of Newton, who, however, had been unable to fix the motion of his own mind.

Thus the language of Pope's claim to have solved the great mystery of character echoes that of Manilius to have unraveled the secrets of the universe, and I hope to show that both his presentation of the problem and his solution are formed on an astrological model. Since Pope elsewhere pokes fun at astrology, it is worth remembering that to the Stoics it was part of the general doctrine of *concordia discors*. Human fates and characters mirrored the ever-changing but always balanced pattern of the heavens.

> When *Nature* order'd this vast Frame to rise,
> *Nature*, the Guardian of these Mysteries,
> And scatter'd Lucid Bodies o'er the Skies;
> When she the *Concave*, whence directly fall
> Streight Lines of Influence round the solid *Ball*,
> Had fill'd with Stars; and made *Earth*, Water, Air,
> And *Fire*, each other mutually repair;
> That Concord might these differing parts controul,
> And Leagues of mutual Aid support the whole;
> That nothing which the *Skies* embrace might be
> From *Heaven*'s supreme Command and Guidance free,
> On *Man* the chiefest Object of her Cares
> Long time she thought, then hung his Fates on *Stars*.
>   [III, 47-58; p. 99]

One would not suppose for a moment that Pope attributed any influence to the stars; but it was not necessary for him to do so in order to accept the image of man's fortune and character as a "well accorded strife" of opposing tendencies.

Before we turn to the doctrine of the ruling passion as it is presented in "To Cobham," let us glance back at its appearance in the *Essay on Man*, not indeed to examine its function in Pope's

argument, but merely to note that there also there seems to be a Manilian influence.

> As Man, perhaps, the moment of his breath,
> Receives the lurking principle of death;
> The young disease, that must subdue at length,
> Grows with his growth, and strengthens with his strength:
> So, cast and mingled with his very frame,
> The Mind's disease, its ruling Passion came.
>
> [II, 133-138]

The opening couplet of this extract carries a suggestion of the important line *"nascentes morimur, finisque ab origine pendet"* (IV, 16), and the remainder recalls the sinister lines quoted in the preceding chapter, which somehow also seem connected with Pope's own long disease:

> The *sixth* but *Twelve* bestows, then Death destroys
> The Parents Hopes, and crops the growing Boys;
> Diseases following, from their Birth create
> A feeble Frame, and fit the Prey for Fate.

Yet the comparison with disease, implying as it does a world without any healthy minds, is perhaps not wholly satisfactory; and the attempt will now be made to show that in "To Cobham" Pope used a different Manilian model. One of the main achievements of Manilian science, perhaps even its culmination, is the reading of natal characters, to which much of the fourth and all of the fifth book are devoted. In Book IV the characters created by the signs of the zodiac are described, and there is also some theoretical discussion of the application of this knowledge to particular births. All this is rather clumsily combined; yet it could still serve Pope's purpose.

First, however, let us briefly consider the position of the "Epistle to Cobham" in Pope's works and in particular how it stands in relation to the *Essay on Man*. This whole question has been discussed at length by Miriam Leranbaum in *Alexander Pope's "Opus Magnum" 1729–1744*, with which most readers

will presumably be familiar. What is important for the present purpose is that Pope was working on "To Cobham" simultaneously with Epistle IV of the *Essay* for some time during 1733, when the first three epistles of the *Essay* had been sent to the press; the two poems appeared within a week of each other in January 1734. "To Cobham" appears to have been intended to occupy an early place in the *Opus Magnum* after the *Essay*, and of the completed poems it is the next after it.

Although "To Cobham" springs largely from Epistle II of the *Essay*, as Leranbaum makes clear, it has, as she also points out, a great deal in common with Epistle IV, with which it was gestated. The attempt will be made to show that it is linked to that epistle by a line of borrowings from Book IV of the *Astronomica*. What is meant by this statement can be seen from a rough outline of part of Book IV (the line numbers of the original and Creech's page numbers are given below):

1. The proem and introductory passage on fate	1–118	2–9
2. A description of primary zodiacal characters	119–293	9–16
3. A description of decans		
a) General theory	294–309	16–17
b) Enumeration	310–362	17–19
c) Their influence on character	363–386	19–20
4. A rhetorical passage on the value of astrology	387–407	20–21
5. The harmful degrees		
a) General theory	408–443	21–22
b) Enumeration	444–501	22–29

I argued in chapter 4 that in Epistle IV of the *Essay*, especially in the first two hundred lines or so, Pope borrowed from section 1 (as above) before turning elsewhere. In "To Cobham" he seems to return to the theoretical parts of Book IV, that is, to sections 3*a*, 3*c*, and 5*a*, which deal with the decans and the harmful degrees.

It should be explained that a decan is a division of ten degrees of the zodiac; and all thirty-six decans are governed by the signs recurring three times in order from Aries. The following table,

which is given in full in Creech's notes, should make matters clearer than the translation, which is slightly inaccurate:

Signs (30° each)	Decans (10°) — governed by
Aries	Aries
	Taurus
	Gemini
Taurus	Cancer
	Leo
	Virgo
Gemini	Libra
	Scorpio
	Sagittarius
Cancer	Capricornus
	Aquarius
	Pisces
Leo	Aries
Etc.	Etc.

The harmful degrees, or parts, are those that through excess of "cold or hot or moist or dry" are unfavorable to their births. There are about a hundred of them scattered throughout the signs in an apparently random way.

Here, then, are extracts from Creech's translation of the description of the decans (which he misleadingly calls "tenths") and of the harmful degrees. I quote section 3*a* of my second table in full and sections 3*b*, 3*c*, and 5*a* in part.

> Thus rule the *Twelve*, these Powers they *singly* own,
> And these would give if they could work alone.
> But none rules *All* its own degrees, they joyn
> Their friendly forces with some other Sign,
> As 'twere compound, and equal parts receive
> From *Other* Signs, as they to *Others* give:
> Thus each hath *Thirty* parts, and each resigns

Two Thirds of those degrees to other Signs:
We call these portions (Art new words will frame,)
The Tenths, the *Number* doth impose the Name:
So hid is Truth, so many Vails o're-spread
Coy *Nature's* Face, and hide her Gloomy Head,
So many are the little Niceties,
So intricate, and puzling are the Skies,
Not easie to be read by common Eyes.
For one appearance in another lies,
Conceals its Powers, and Acts in a Disguise;
And that which *Lurks*, and subtly interferes
Hath different *Powers* from that which then appears.
Not Day, but piercing Thought must clear this Sky,
The Labour of thy *Mind*, not of thy *Eye*;
Press bravely on, and pass the Gloomy Cloud,
Enter, and view the inside of the *God*;
The Path is dark, and lest thy Mind should stray
I'll boldly lead, and shew the nearest way;
I'll Sing what League the different Parts combines,
And shew how others Rule in other Signs.
                                        [IV, 292-311; pp. 16-17]

    This thing consider'd well thy Mind prepares
To know the secret guidance of the Stars;
They *interchange* their Powers, they mix their Laws,
And all agree to make one Common Cause;
For these *Divisions* do unite the Sky,
The more they *part* the *closer* is the Tye.
    But now, lest Error should thy Mind surprise,
Believe not the *Appearance* of the Skies;
They make a shew, they spread a Glaring Light
To lead thee on, but never guide thee right;
Let *Active Thought* assisting Sense pursue
Coy Truth's retreat, and take an open view:
What ever Things are born, their Minds receive
The fatal Temper which that Sign can give
That governs in the *Tenths*, the Foreign Ray,
Tempers the Mass, and forms the easie Clay.
    A Thousand Reasons for this Truth appear
From *different* Births belonging to *One* Star;
Of all those Creatures, that at once do see

The Light, scarce Two can perfectly agree;
But different Tempers all the shapes adorn,
As various as the Bodies that are born:
For though one *Chiefly* Rules, yet others *joyn*
And change the *proper* influence of that Sign:
These Interchanges all our Thoughts distract,
We think on other Signs, whilst others Act.
    Thus neither *singly* will the *Ram* bestow
A love to Cloathing, nor the *Bull* to plough.

[IV, 363-380; p. 19]

    Observe the numerous parts of the *Degrees*
What *Heat* doth scorch or what the *Cold* doth freeze,
(Unfruitful both) where *too much Moisture* flows,
Or *Drought* doth drain, and various Fates dispose:
    For different Qualities in Signs controul,
There's nought all-over-equal in the whole.
For view the *Earth*, the gliding Streams, or Flood,
Faults are on all sides, Bad is mixt with Good.
Thus *Barren* Seasons midst the *Best* appear,
And a small Turn blasts all the Blooming Year.
A *Port* turns *Shelf*, and the inglorious Sand
Forfeits that Praise which once its Safety gain'd.
Now Streams through Plains in *smooth Meanders* play,
Then Roar o're Rocks, and force a *rugged* way.
Such *Inequality* above appears,
And thus the Sky is vary'd in the Stars;
As Sign from Sign, so from it self the same
Doth disagree, and spread unequal Flame;
And Signs, whose *Sovereign* influence Births do find
In *One* degree, are in the next *unkind*:
Those things these parts o're-rule, no Joys shall know
Or little Pleasure *over-mixt* with Woe.

[IV, 410-430; pp. 21-22]

The gulf in tone and manner between these crabbed passages and Pope's brilliant and worldly poem is so great that it may seem wild to suggest an affinity; yet if we consider the substance, it may seem less improbable. Manilius, like Pope, is developing a theory of human character. The decans imply that there is one main un-

derlying lifelong influence, obscured, perhaps, by other, less fundamental influences — a doctrine not so very different from the ruling passion. Furthermore, Manilius's theories, as we have seen, are rooted in cosmic harmony, which is the basis of Pope's whole philosophy. Even the theory of the harmful degrees, from which Pope no doubt largely out of opportunism seems to have drawn some material, posits a lack of balance in the opposites and so fits well with Pope's views.

If now we look again at Pope's exposition of the problem of character in the first part of the "Epistle to Cobham," we shall find that there seem to be certain detailed points of resemblance to the Manilian passages. One may attempt to demonstrate this with the following example:

> And yet the fate of all extremes is such,
> Men may be read, as well as Books too much.
> To Observations which ourselves we make,
> We grow more partial for th' observer's sake;
> To written Wisdom, as another's, less:
> Maxims are drawn from Notions, these from Guess.
>
> [9-14]

Pope here makes a distinction between direct impressions and thought, between our own reading of men and our own observations and books and maxims. In Manilius we find something, at least, of the same distinction,

> But now, lest Error should thy Mind surprise,
> Believe not the *Appearance* of the Skies;
> They make a shew, they spread a Glaring Light
> To lead thee on, but never guide thee right;
> Let *Active Thought* assisting Sense pursue
> Coy Truth's retreat, and take an open view;

and compare also

> Not Day, but piercing Thought must clear this Sky,
> The Labour of thy *Mind*, not of thy *Eye*.

Pope continues,

> There's some Peculiar in each leaf and grain,
> Some unmark'd fibre, or some varying vein,
>
> [15-16]

stressing how even very small parts of nature are distinguished by differences that may be almost unnoticeable ("unmarked") in their own yet smaller parts. Manilius has this,

> So many are the little Niceties,
> So intricate, and puzling are the Skies,
> Not easie to be read by common Eyes,

stressing the subtleties that make the stars difficult to interpret and which distinguish one birth from another. Pope's next couplet, also,

> Shall only Man be taken in the gross?
> Grant but as many sorts of Mind as Moss,
>
> [17-18]

emphasizes the multiplicity of differences in human beings, and the same point is made in

> Of all those Creatures, that at once do see
> The Light, scarce Two can perfectly agree;
> But different Tempers all the shapes adorn,
> As various as the Bodies that are born.

Pope's following couplet, again,

> That each from other differs, first confess;
> Next, that he varies from himself no less,
>
> [19-20]

closely resembles this couplet from the passage on the harmful degrees.

> As Sign from Sign, so from itself the same
> Doth disagree, and spread unequal Flame,

which translates a line perhaps even closer to Pope, *"ut signum a signo, sic a se discrepat ipsum."* (The parallels from Montaigne and others quoted in the Twickenham edition are also remarkably close.) A few lines lower down, we find these observations on human mutability over time,

> Our depths who fathoms, or our shallows finds,
> Quick whirls, and shifting eddies, of our minds?
> Life's stream for Observation will not stay,
> It hurries all too fast to mark their way,
>
> [29-32]

which by their images of navigational hazards in the first couplet, followed by swift streams in the second, seem to recall these on mutability:

> A *Port* turns *Shelf*, and the inglorious Sand
> Forfeits that Praise which once its Safety gain'd.
> Now Streams through Plains in *smooth Meanders* play,
> Then roar o're Rocks, and force a *rugged* way.

In these, then, and in other possible resemblances that I do not retail, we seem to see a Manilian contribution to Pope's statement of the problem of reading human nature. After examining further argument and illustration, we reach Pope's solution, the doctrine of the ruling passion. It has already been suggested that in this "Epistle" Pope presents this doctrine in terms of Manilian science. The main inspiration appears to have been provided by the theory of the decans. The relationship between the main zodiacal signs and the decans is the model for that between the ruling passions and the "second qualities" that can obscure them. First, let us see the lines in which the doctrine is introduced:

> Search then the Ruling Passion: There alone,
> The Wild are constant, and the Cunning known;
> The Fool consistent, and the False sincere;
> Priests, Princes, Women, no dissemblers here.
> This clue once found, unravels all the rest,
> The prospect clears, and Wharton stands confest.
>
> [174-179]

This exhortation may be compared with

> Not Day, but piercing Thought must clear this Sky,
> The Labour of thy *Mind*, not of thy *Eye*;
> Press bravely on, and pass the Gloomy Cloud,
> Enter, and View the inside of the *God*;
> . . . .
> I'll sing what League the different Parts combines,
> And show how others Rule in other Signs.

In each of these passages the reader is urged to mental effort, which will give him the key to the mystery — the "prospect will clear" or thought "will clear this sky." After his character of Wharton, Pope continues,

> Yet, in this search, the wisest may mistake,
> If second qualities for first they take,
>
> [210-211]

a couplet that contains the essence of the doctrine of the ruling passion and seems to be modeled on lines that similarly contain the core of the doctrine of the decans:

> For though one *Chiefly* Rules, yet others *joyn*
> And change the *proper* influence of that Sign:
> These Interchanges all our Thoughts distract,
> We think on other Signs, whilst others Act.

"The wisest may mistake" parallels in sense (showing intellect deceived by appearances) "all our Thoughts distract," and "If second qualities for first they take" seems to be a paraphrase of "We think on other Signs, whilst others Act." Creech's Latin idiom in this line may obscure his meaning, which is that we cannot easily tell whether it is the influence of the basic natal sign or of the sign that governs the decan which will be effective. It is natural for Pope to speak of first and second qualities if he has in mind Creech's table, with its first and second columns showing the basic signs and the signs of the decans respectively. Furthermore, the word *rule* used by Creech in this context may be significant — he uses it over a dozen times in his description of the decans and

synonyms such as "govern" some eight or nine times. This might
perhaps have suggested to Pope the use of the decans as a model
for the ruling passion (a phrase that Pope did not invent but
which already existed, as the note on page 71 of the Twickenham
Essay on Man points out).

Later Pope tells us that the ruling passion remains unchanged throughout our lives:

> In this one Passion man can strength enjoy,
> As Fits give vigour, just when they destroy.
> Time, that on all things lays his lenient hand,
> Yet tames not this; it sticks to our last sand.
> Consistent in our follies and our sins,
> Here honest Nature ends as she begins.
>
> [222-227]

These lines, which are illustrated in the anecdotes at the end of the
poem, also have something in common with the zodiacal theory
of character, for they too show the influence of "nascentes morimur finisque ab origine pendet" or in Creech's expanded translation,

> *As we are Born we Dye, our Lots are cast,*
> *And our first Hour disposeth of our last.*

Were it not for this lifelong persistence, Manilius's and Pope's
theories would both fall to the ground.

These resemblances are mostly tenuous, but their combined
effect, and that of the cosmological references with which they are
introduced and of Pope's allusions to the important line *nascentes morimur*, go, in my view, well beyond anything that could
reasonably be ascribed to chance and therefore seem to establish
this part of Book IV of the *Astronomica* as a source of "To Cobham." The doctrinal value of the source was, I believe, considerable, since there is difficulty in reconciling the aim of achieving a
well-accorded strife of the passions, which Pope urges on us in the
Essay on Man, with the hypothesis that in every man a "master-
passion swallows all the rest." However, the theory of the decans

provides a model of how "one chiefly rules yet others join" while being firmly rooted in the doctrine of *concordia discors* which pervades the whole *Astronomica* and, as the lines previously quoted from Book III show, forms the basis of astrology:

> That Concord might these differing parts controul,
> And Leagues of mutual Aid support the whole
> . . . .
> On *Man* the chiefest Object of her Cares
> Long time she thought, then hung his Fates on *Stars*.

If this thesis is correct, it would imply that after discarding the astrology, Pope has been able to create in "To Cobham," for all its light and fashionable tone, a study of man's nature in terms of the changing appearances but underlying ordered immutability of the universe; in other words, it is a poem in which psychology becomes a branch of cosmology and microcosm is related to macrocosm. This would perhaps help to vindicate Pope in his claim to an original theory.

APPENDIX

"A Lady's Grotto"

The following poem was printed in *Spectator* No. 632 of 13 December 1714 as the enclosure to a reader's letter signed A. B. and dated in Dublin 30 November. It will be remembered that the *Spectator* had originally closed down in 1712 but was revived by Addison for a few months in 1714 before its final closure; No. 632 was almost the last issue.

To Mrs. _____ on her *Grotto*.
A Grotto *so compleat, with such Design,*
What Hands, Calypso, *cou'd have form'd but Thine?*
Each chequer'd Pebble, and each shining Shell,
So well proportion'd, and dispos'd so well,
Surprizing Lustre from thy Thought receive,
Assuming Beauties more than Nature gave.
To Her their various Shapes, and glossy Hue,
Their curious Symmetry they owe to You.
Not fam'd Amphion's *Lute, whose pow'rful Call*
Made willing Stones dance to the Theban Wall,
In more harmonious Ranks cou'd make them fall.
Not Ev'ning Cloud a brighter Arch can shew,
Nor richer Colours paint the heav'nly Bow.

Where can unpolished Nature boast a Piece,
In all her Mossie Cells exact as This?
At the gay parti-colour'd Scene we start,
For Chance too regular, too rude for Art.

157

> *Charm'd with the sight, my ravish'd Breast is fir'd*
> *With Hints like those which ancient Bards inspir'd;*
> *All the feign'd Tales by Superstition told,*
> *All the bright Train of fabled Nymphs of Old,*
> *Th' enthusiastick Muse believes are true,*
> *Thinks the Spot sacred, and its Genius You.*
> *Lost in wild Rapture, wou'd she fain disclose,*
> *How by degrees the pleasing Wonder rose;*
> *Industrious in a faithful Verse to trace*
> *The various Beauties of the lovely Place:*
> *And while she keeps the glowing Work in view,*
> *Thro' ev'ry Maze thy artful Hand pursue.*
>
> *Oh were I equal to the bold Design,*
> *Or cou'd I boast such happy Art as Thine!*
> *That cou'd rude Shells in such sweet Order place,*
> *Give common Objects such uncommon Grace!*
> *Like them my well chose Words in ev'ry Line,*
> *As sweetly temper'd, shou'd as sweetly shine.*
> *So just a Fancy shou'd my Numbers warm,*
> *Like the gay Piece shou'd the Description charm.*
> *Then with superior Strength my Voice I'd raise,*
> *The echoing Grotto shou'd approve my Lays,*
> *Pleas'd to reflect the well sung Founder's Praise.*

It is plain enough that this account of an artistic arrangement of pebbles and shells, which may be meant to represent earth and water, is a Creation passage like many we have seen in Pope. Many detailed resemblances may be traced, as we may see in the following examination of specific words and phrases in particular lines.

1,30. "Design" is a favorite word of Pope's in Creation passages, carrying as it does the implication of controlling mind and purpose. Compare, for example, *Essay on Criticism*, "when the faithful *Pencil* has design'd" (484); *To Mr. Jervas*, "whether thy hands strike out some free design" (3); *To Burlington*, "Till Kings call forth th' Idea's of your mind, Proud to accomplish what such hands design'd" (195-196), or, in reversal, "random drawings [*disegni*]" (27). With "bold design" in line 30 compare *Essay on Criticism*, "he checks the bold Design" (136).

2. "Hands" — compare the references to hands in the preceding note and also in *Essay on Criticism*, "Nature waits upon his Hand" (487). "Calypso" — Homer's Calypso was not only a grotto dweller but also an artist since she wove and sang and probably also gardened.

3. The contrasting adjectives emphasize the variety of the materials and their *concordia discors*. Compare the description of the rivers in *Windsor Forest*.

4. "Well proportion'd" — compare the "well-proportion'd dome" (247) in *Essay on Criticism* and its Ovidian origins. "Dispos'd so well" — compare Sandys's "thus orderly dispos'd."

5. "Lustre from thy Thought" — compare *Essay on Criticism*, "Some *bright Idea* of the Master's Mind" (485); *To Mr. Jervas*, "fair ideas . . . in the picture glow" (43-44). Pope often mentions light in Creation contexts, presumably alluding to Genesis.

6,14. For the improvement of nature compare "*Nature* to Advantage drest" (*Essay on Criticism*, 297).

10. "Willing" — "joins willing woods" (*To Burlington*, 62). "Dance" — a harmonious motion — "those move easiest who have learn'd to dance" (*Essay on Criticism*, 363).

11. "Harmonious Ranks" — Peterborough arranged Pope's vines in ranks (*Imitations of Horace, Satire, II, i*, 130).

16. "Parti-colour'd Scene" — compare "checquer'd Scene" (*Windsor Forest*, 17).

17. "Chance . . . Art" — as my text has shown, this opposition is one of Pope's basic cosmological preoccupations.

18. With this line, compare Sandys's "Nature, who, with ravisht eye, Affects his owne-made Beauties." Our poet's breast is ravished at the sight of the beauty Calypso has made. We have seen that Pope imitates these lines, as in *To Burlington*, "The suff'ring eye inverted Nature sees" (119). "My ravish'd Breast is fir'd" — compare *Windsor Forest*, "were my Breast inspir'd with equal Flame" (9).

22. "Enthusiastick" — to be taken certainly not in its modern sense nor, I think, in its original sense of "possessed by a god" but in its more ordinary contemporary sense of enthusiasm in religion. This witty stroke may remind us of Dryden.

23. A reference to the *genius loci* — compare *To Burlington*, "Consult the Genius of the Place" (57), but our poet's ear was far too good for "place sacred."

25. This line is closely paralleled by *To Burlington*, "Time shall make it grow / A Work to wonder at" (69-70). This is a most potent resemblance, especially in combination with the mention of the *genius loci* in each poem. As I have explained in the text, I believe that Pope's many references to the wonders of divine or human creation are a response to the Manilian *solvitque animis miracula rerum*. Compare *Essay on Criticism*, "*with Reason* to *Admire*" (101), "The World's just Wonder" (248), and "th' admiring Eyes" (250); *Rape of the Lock*, "the Wonders of her Face" (142); *Essay on Man*, "th' amazing whole" (I, 247); and *To Burlington* "your admiration call" (113), "Erect new wonders" (192).

28–29. The Muse admires the parts but does not lose sight of the whole, unlike Bentley and the other scholar-dunces of *Dunciad*, IV, 235.

32. "To place in order" is *digerere*; hence, this line forms an allusion to the *rudis indigestaque moles*.

34–37. Pope compares his own art to Creation in *Imitations of Horace, Epistles*, II, ii, 153 ff., where he discusses, among other things, his choice of words.

35. "Temper'd" — compare Ovid's *temperiemque dedit*, often imitated by Pope, as my text has shown.

38–40. Pope's Creation passages often end with, or contain, a reference to satisfaction and praise. Compare *Rape of the Lock*, "Betty's prais'd" (I, 148); *Dunciad*, "With self-applause" (I, 82), and other references easily found. With the praise echoed by the pleased grotto, compare *To Bathurst*, "Pleas'd Vaga echoes . . . Severn hoarse applause resounds" (251-252).

39. This reads like a translation of a line by Sannazaro, "et percussa meis vocibus antra sonant," from an elegy that Pope later included in his *Selecta Poemata Italorum* of 1740 (Vol. II, p. 1). It was not in Atterbury's collection of 1684 which formed the nucleus of Pope's.

My own opinion might as well be declared: that is, that the poem is by Pope. If so, the Dublin date must be a stratagem, no doubt to conceal his authorship better, though we can only guess why he should have wanted to do so. The versification seems good enough to have been his and is not far from being too good for anybody else — the opening of the third paragraph, in particular, seems to have his own matchless harmony.

If it is his, it seems like early work. Its fault as a Creation poem is that it does not describe the grotto so as to bring out its artistic *concordia discors* but relies too much on exclamation; yet it still reads almost like a preparatory sketch for the passage beginning "Consult the Genius of the Place" with which it has several parallels and where, after an apt description, the exclamation is reduced to one effective last line.

If the poem is not Pope's, it seems to me yet more interesting as an elaborate exercise in his cosmological manner by an imitator who seems to have been well acquainted with some of Pope's more recondite reading and whose work Pope in his turn imitated in later poems. Although Knapp's verses in Pope's 1717 volume were also dated in Ireland and although Knapp seems to have known Addison, this poem surely cannot be by him or at least not by him unaided, for it is well beyond his powers. Here then would be a further piece of evidence for the understanding of Pope's cosmological writing by his contemporaries.

Notes

Chap 1: Introduction

    1. For Pope's library, see Professor Mack's article "Pope's Books" in *English Literature in the Age of Disguise*, edited by Maximillian E. Novak.

  2: The Rape of a Myth

    1. The structural similarities are more apparent in the 1712 edition, in which Canto II began with the ten lines that begin Canto IV in the revised poem and then continued with what is now line 93 of Canto IV.

    2. Pope's words are in fact closer to a couplet on meteors from the *Astronomica*:

Some *equally diffus'd*, like flaming Hair,
Draw fiery Tresses through the Liquid Air.
                        [I, 835-837; p. 33]

The references to hair in Ovid and Manilius were too apt for him to miss.

  3: The Wild Heap and the Ordered Frame

    1. Here is the original (I have transliterated the Greek words):

Status rerum perturbatus . . . Plutarchus [akosmian] *vocavit statum reip. Rom. qui erat tempore belli civilis, cui* [eukosmian] *opponit. Apud Aristotelem autem* [akosmian] *Bud. vertit Congeriem confusam et inconditam, in lib. De mundo . . . haec enim verba sic reddit. Universumque*

> *ipsum commodius* [kosmon] *nominaveris, id est*
> *compagem rerum compositam concinnoque or-*
> *dine digestam, quam* [akosmian], *id est conge-*
> *riem confusam et inconditam.*

2. The original is as follows:

> *Secerno, Discerno, Dirimo. Primam enim hanc*
> *esse puto verbi* [krino] *significationem, non au-*
> *tem eam qua pro Iudico ponitur, quin potius*
> *hanc ex illa profectam. ut videlicet* [krinein] *dic-*
> *tum sit pro* [krinein neikea] *(quod ipsum et apud*
> *Homerum legitur) id est Dirimere lites. nam qui*
> *iudicat, lites dirimit.*

3. See *De Architectura*, Book I, Chapter II.

4. See *De Architectura*, Book III, Chapter I.

5. For a full discussion of this subject, see Rudolf
    Wittkower's *Architectural Principles in the Age of
    Humanism.*

6. "All-devouring" was replaced by "all-involving"
    in 1744.

7. This interpretation of the description of the
    gardens can strengthen the view that Timon is a
    satire upon Walpole (though not only that) In
    many of his Creation passages, Pope refers to the
    appearance in the thing created of the "image" of
    the creator's mind; it is often "seen" or "beheld."
    Given that one nickname of Walpole was the
    "Wall," as Mack shows (*The Garden and the City*,
    Appendix F), this reference can be found in "On
    ev'ry side you look, behold the Wall!" That is,
    wherever you look, you see the image or imprint of
    Walpole's mind. The wall is also a gardening
    fault, making it impossible to call in the country
    or to vary and conceal the bounds. (The Hanover-
    ian palace at Herrenhausen was another most
    conspicuous offender against these instructions;
    see illustration 7 in Ragnhild Hatton's *George I:
    Elector and King.*) Another possible reference to

Walpole may lie in the phrase "puny insect." It is borrowed from Creech's Lucretius:

E'en now the World's grown old; e'en she that bore
Such mighty bulky *Animals* before,
Now bears a *Puny* insect, and no more.

[II, 1151]

Walpole, although he might seem a puny insect at Houghton, is well described as a mighty bulky animal.

8. This and other passages have been influenced by *Mundus Muliebris: or the Ladies Dressing-Room Unlock'd and her Toilette Spread*, a charming and witty little poem and a treasury of fashion terms, published anonymously in 1690 but attributable at least in part to John Evelyn's daughter Mary who had died, while still in her teens, in 1683.

9. This note is adapted from a sentence of Creech's preface (pp. 61-62) describing the Stoic philosophy. By attributing the theory to the Epicureans (it was common to both schools), Pope can use it to satirize materialism.

10. Emrys Jones, in his British Academy lecture "Pope and Dulness," quotes Creech's lines.

11. Searle's complete description is reproduced in Mack's *The Garden and the City*, Appendix C. One suspects Pope's hand behind Searle's.

12. This interpretation owes much to Thomas E. Maresca's *Pope's Horatian Poems*.

Chap. 4: Manilius, Creech, and *An Essay on Man*

1. In *Alexander Pope: The Poetry of Allusion*. The chapter on the *Essay* is called "The Scale of Wonder," pp. 206-240.

2. Compare also, for example, "The *World*'s just Wonder" (*Essay on Criticism*, 248) and "Erect new

wonders" (*To Burlington*, 192), both places where Pope emphasizes the marvel of creation, albeit human creation.

3. In *Newton Demands the Muse*.

4. Pope here differs from his admired Sandys, who has, "And what, ô you Gods, is of all most ridiculous, *Erigone* hath brought her dog with her; least she should be sad, and want her old companion in heaven" (p. 109).

5. Compare especially a couplet of Creech's invention near the opening of the *Astronomica*:

> My verse shall sing what various *Aspect* reigns
> When *Kings* are doom'd to Crowns and *Slaves* to
> Chains.
>
> [p. 3]

6. Compare another of Creech's additions to the opening of the *Astronomica*,

> I'll find what Sign and Constellation rule,
> And make the difference 'twixt the Wise and Fool.
>
> [p. 3]

Works Cited or Referred to

Note: all the classical texts listed are in the Loeb Classical Library.

Battestin, Martin Carey. *The Providence of Wit: Aspects of Form in Augustan Literature and the Arts*. Oxford: Clarendon Press, 1974.

Brower, Reuben Arthur. *Alexander Pope: the Poetry of Allusion*. Oxford: Clarendon Press, 1969. ?

Cowley, Abraham. *The English Writings of Abraham Cowley*. Edited by A. R. Waller. Cambridge: Cambridge University Press, 1905-06.

Creech, Thomas. *The Five Books of M. Manilius, Containing a System of the Ancient Astronomy and Astrology*. London, 1697.

———. *T. Lucretius Carus. "De Natura Rerum."* London, 1682.

Cumberland, Bishop Richard. *Sanchoniatho's Phoenician History Translated from the First Book of Eusebius De Praeparatione Evangelica*. London, 1720.

Denham, Sir John. *The Poetical Works of Sir John Denham*. Edited by Theodore Howard Banks Jr. New Haven: Yale University Press; London: Oxford University Press, 1928.

Desaguliers, John Theophilus. *The Newtonian System of the World the Best Model of Government: an Allegorical Poem*. London, 1728.

Dryden, John. *The Poems of John Dryden*. Edited by John Sargeaunt. London: Oxford University Press, 1956.

Estienne, Henri (Stephanus). *Thesaurus Graecae Linguae*. Geneva, 1572.

Evelyn, Mary. *Mundus Muliebris: or, the Ladies Dressing-Room Unlock'd, and her Toilette Spread. In Burlesque*. London, 1690.

Grotius, Hugo. *De Veritate Religionis Christianae*. Leyden, 1627.

Hatton, Ragnhild. *George I: Elector and King*. London: Thames and Hudson, 1978.

Hesiod. *Hesiod, the Homeric Hymns and Homerica*. Edited and translated by H. G. Evelyn-White. London: William Heinemann; Cambridge: Harvard University Press, 1936.

Hobbes, Thomas. *Leviathan*. Oxford: Basil Blackwell, 1946.

Homer. *Iliad*. Edited and translated by A. T. Murray. London: William Heinemann; New York: G P Putnam's Sons, 1924-25.

————. *Odyssey*. Edited and translated by A. T. Murray. London: William Heinemann; New York: G. P. Putnam's Sons, 1919.

Horace. *Satires, Epistles and Ars Poetica*. Edited and translated by H. R. Fairclough. London: William Heinemann; New York: G. P. Putnam's Sons, 1926.

Johnson, Samuel. *Lives of the English Poets*. London: Oxford University Press, 1964.

Jones, Emrys. "Pope and Dulness." In *Pope: a Collection of Critical Essays*. Edited by J. V. Guerinot. Englewood Cliffs: Prentice-Hall, 1972.

Jones, William Powell. *The Rhetoric of Science: a Study of Scientific Ideas and Imagery in Eighteenth-Century English Poetry*. Berkeley: University of California Press, 1966, pp. 124-157.

Leranbaum, Miriam. *Alexander Pope's "Opus Magnum" 1729-1744*. Oxford: Clarendon Press, 1977.

Lucretius. *De Rerum Natura*. Edited and translated by W. H. D. Rouse. London: William Heinemann; New York: G. P. Putnam's Sons, 1924.

————. See also Creech, Thomas.

Mack, Maynard. "Pope's Books: a Biographical Survey with a Finding List." In *English Literature in the Age of Disguise*. Edited by Maximillian Erwin Novak. Berkeley: University of California Press, 1977, pp. 209-305.

————. *The Garden and the City: Retirement and Politics in the Later Poetry of Pope, 1731-1743*. Toronto: University of Toronto Press, 1969.

Manilius. *Astronomica*. Edited and translated by G. P. Goold. Cambridge: Harvard University Press; London: William Heinemann, 1977.

————. See also Creech, Thomas and Sherburne, Sir Edward.

Maresca, Thomas E. *Pope's Horatian Poems*. Columbia: Ohio State University Press, 1966.

Newton, Sir Isaac. *Philosophiae Naturalis Principia Mathematica*. London, 1687.

Nicholson, Marjorie Hope. *Newton Demands the Muse: Newton's Opticks and the Eighteenth Century Poets*. Princeton: Princeton University Press, 1946.

Ovid. *Metamorphoses*. Edited and translated by Frank Justus Miller. London: William Heinemann; Cambridge: Harvard University Press, 1946.

————. See also Sandys, George.

Pope, Alexander. *The Poems of Alexander Pope*. General Editor, John Butt. London: Methuen and Co.; New Haven: Yale University Press, 1939-69.

———. ed. *Selecta Poemata Italorum qui Latine Scripserunt*. London, 1740.

Sanchuniathon. See Cumberland, Bishop Richard.

Sandys, George. *A Paraphrase upon the Psalms of David*. London, 1676.

———. *Ovid's Metamorphosis Englished, Mythologiz'd, and Represented in Figures*. Oxford, 1632.

Sellar, William Young. *The Roman Poets of the Augustan Age: Horace and the Elegiac Poets*. Oxford: Clarendon Press, 1899.

Shakespeare, William. *The Works of Shakespeare*. Edited by Arthur Henry Bullen. Oxford: Shakespeare Head Press, 1934.

Sherburne, Sir Edward. *The Sphere of Marcus Manilius Made an English Poem*. London, 1675.

Spectator, The. Edited by Gregory Smith. London: Dent; New York: Dutton, 1970.

Spence, Joseph. *Observations, Anecdotes, and Characters of Books and Men, Collected from Conversation*. Edited by James Marshall Osborn. Oxford: Clarendon Press, 1966.

Spenser, Edmund. *Poetical Works*. Edited by J. C. Smith and E. de Selincourt. London: Oxford University Press, 1966.

Stanley, Thomas. *The History of Philosophy*. London, 1701.

———. *The History of the Chaldaick Philosophy*. London, 1701.

Stephanus. See Estienne, Henri.

Vitruvius. *On Architecture*. Edited and translated by Frank Granger. New York: G. P. Putnam's Sons; London: William Heinemann, 1931-34.

Wasserman, Earl Reeves. *The Subtler Language: Critical Readings of Neoclassic and Romantic Poems*. Baltimore: John Hopkins Press, 1959.

Wittkower, Rudolf. *Architectural Principles in the Age of Humanism*. London: Tiranti, 1962.

Index